SPECTRUM®

Spelling

Grade 4

Published by Spectrum®
an imprint of Carson-Dellosa Publishing LLC
Greensboro, NC

Spectrum®
An imprint of Carson-Dellosa Publishing LLC
P.O. Box 35665
Greensboro, NC 27425 USA

ISBN 978-0-7696-5264-1

09-296127811

Table of Contents Grade 4

Table of Contents, continued

Lesson 2 Words with the Short **i**, **o**, and **u** Sounds

Words in Writing

Write a description of a chore that you do at home. Use at least two words from the box.

_____

_____

_____

exit	suggest	river	inspect	umbrella	multiple	prism
bottom	polish	closet	possible	window	intersect	column
electric	until	victim	distance	finish		

Dictionary Practice

Write the words from the box in the groups where they belong. Some words belong in more than one group.

/i/ Sound

_____   _____   _____

_____   _____   _____

_____   _____   _____

_____   _____

_____

/o/ Sound   ### /u/ Sound

_____   _____

_____   _____

_____   _____

_____   _____

_____

Lesson 3 Words with **scr**, **squ**, **str**, and **thr**

Say each word. Listen to the beginning sounds. Then, write the word.

Spelling Tip	The letters **scr**, **squ**, **str**, and **thr** spell the beginning consonant sounds of some words.

Spelling Words

throne _____

stretch _____

squirm _____

throw _____

strap _____

through _____

scream _____

streak _____

squeaky _____

strength _____

thrill _____

scrape _____

threat _____

screw _____

string _____

Lesson 3 Words with scr, squ, str, and thr

Words in Context

Write the missing spelling words.

Take a Deep Breath!

Challenge

Circle the other words with **scr**, **squ**, **str**, and **thr**.

Ride the Maximum Force roller coaster

for the _____ of a lifetime! The moment you squeeze into

a car and buckle your safety _____, you'll begin to

_____ nervously in your seat. The metal

wheels of the cars will slowly _____ along

the rails as you move upward. On the first hill, the ride

will stop for a moment. You will feel like a king sitting on

his _____ as you look out on the grounds

of the park that _____ out before you.

All of a sudden, the cars will jolt forward and nearly

_____ you out of your seat. The cars will _____

along the track like lightning. As you seem to fly _____ the

air, you will hang onto the safety bar with all of your _____.

Your throat will be so dry with fright that you won't even be able to

_____. But don't worry—there is no _____ of

danger. Although the cables sound _____ and are no

thicker than a _____, they're made of steel. Every latch,

cable, and _____ on the ride is secure.

Lesson 3 Words with **scr**, **squ**, **str**, and **thr**

Fun with Words

Write the spelling word that rhymes with each underlined word.

1. It's quite a _____ to run down the <u>hill</u>.

2. I started to _____ when I had a bad <u>dream</u>.

3. When you pull on the _____, the bell will <u>ring</u>.

4. I touched the <u>worm</u>, and it started to _____.

5. Why did you _____ the skin off the <u>grape</u>?

6. The queen was <u>alone</u> as she sat on her _____.

7. Why did you _____ the ball in the <u>snow</u>?

8. Please fasten the _____ across your <u>lap</u>.

9. The boys used all their _____ to run the last <u>length</u>.

10. The old stairs are <u>creaky</u>, and they're also _____.

Words Across the Curriculum

Say each science word. Then, write the word.

1. squid   _____   3. squash   _____

2. straw   _____   4. throat   _____

Write the science word that belongs with each group of words.

1. grass, wheat, hay, _____

2. chin, _____, neck, chest

3. potato, lettuce, tomato, _____

4. octopus, _____, jellyfish, sponge

Lesson 3 Words with scr, squ, str, and thr

Words in Writing

Write an ad for a ride or other attraction that you think is exciting. ~~Use at least four words from the box.~~

Come buy some of our lovely roses @ cece's rose shop on 6th street! We are open from 7:45 until around 5:00! We sell roses in boursts off beautiful colors. drop by and have a look see to-day!

throne	throw	scream	strength	threat	squid	straw
stretch	strap	streak	thrill	screw	squash	throat
squirm	through	squeaky	scrape	string		

Misspelled Words

Read the ad and circle the five misspelled words. Then, write the words correctly on the lines below.

Halloween is almost here, so be sure to visit the Haunted House. As you walk thruogh the dark, skweeky house, you will have one scary threll after another. You will experience spooky sounds and sights that will stretch your imagination. Try not to skream as the giant worms sqirm all around you!

_____ _____ _____

_____ _____

Lesson 4 Words with **ch** and **sh**

Say each word. Listen for the /ch/ and /sh/ sounds. Then, write the word.

Spelling Tip	The /ch/ sound is often spelled **ch**. The /sh/ sound is often spelled **sh**.

Spelling Words

bunch   _____

cheese   _____

hunch   _____

shift   _____

charge   _____

perch   _____

ranch   _____

pinch   _____

cherry   _____

sheep   _____

punch   _____

cheap   _____

shelter   _____

chief   _____

chance   _____

Lesson 4 Words with **ch** and **sh**

Words in Context

Write the missing spelling words.

Agriculture in California

> **Challenge**
>
> Circle the other words with /ch/ and /sh/.

California is the _____

agricultural state. Crops are produced on a farm, while animals are raised

on a _____. Orange, _____, and peach

trees thrive in the hot days. The chilly nights give them a

_____ to recover from the heat.

During the harvest, every fruit picker works a

long _____ from morning to evening.

Workers climb trees and _____

on the lower branches to reach the fruit.

Some workers _____ over

shrubs to pick blueberries and raspberries.

Others carefully pick each _____ of grapes from its vine.

Later, other workers take the grapes to a covered _____

and _____ the grapes from their stems. Some of the grapes

are made into juice and fruit _____.

Cows and _____ are also raised in California, so the

prices that the ranchers _____ for dairy products, including

milk and _____, are _____ there.

Lesson 4 Words with **ch** and **sh**

Fun with Words

Write the spelling word that answers the question "What am I?"

1. You need food, water and me to survive.
   What am I?   _____

2. Horses and cattle live on me. What am I?   _____

3. I can mean a change or a time period of work.
   What am I?   _____

4. I can be positive, negative, or neutral. What am I? _____

5. I can be a group of bananas or grapes. What am I? _____

6. I am a leader of people or the main thing.
   What am I?   _____

7. I am a fruit and a popular flavor. What am I?   _____

8. You might like me best when I'm melted.
   What am I?   _____

Words Across the Curriculum

Say each language arts word. Then, write the word.

1. chapter _____   3. publish _____

2. research_____   4. English _____

Write the language arts word that fits each group of words.

1. edit, proofread, _____

2. paragraph, page, _____

3. French, Spanish, _____

4. references, sources, _____

Lesson 4 Words with **ch** and **sh**

Words in Writing

Write a short report about some goods that are produced in your state. Use at least four words from the box.

_____

_____

_____

_____

_____

bunch	shift	ranch	sheep	shelter	chapter	research
cheese	charge	pinch	punch	chief	publish	English
hunch	perch	cherry	cheap	chance		

Misspelled Words

Read the paragraph from a report. Circle the five misspelled words. Then, write the words correctly on the lines below.

   I did some researsh about some foods and animals that are raised on farms in Wisconsin. Cows, hogs, and sheap make up most of the livestock raised in the state. A huge amount of milk, chease, and other dairy products are produced there, so these products are fairly cheep for the people of this state. I was surprised to find that Wisconsin farmers grow a large number of chery trees. However, apples are their chief fruit crop.

_____   _____   _____

_____   _____

Lesson 5 Silent Letters: Words with **gn**, **mb**, **tch**, and **wr**

Say each word. Listen to the sound of each consonant diagraph and notice which letter is silent. Then, write the word.

Spelling Tip	The consonant diagraphs **gn**, **mb**, **tch**, and **wr** each have a silent letter. In the consonant diagraph **gn**, the **g** is silent. In the consonant diagraph **mb**, the **b** is silent. In the consonant diagraph **tch**, the **t** is silent. In the consonant blend **wr**, the **w** is silent.

Spelling Words

fetch   _____

wren   _____

sketch   _____

design   _____

wreck   _____

comb   _____

twitch   _____

wrinkle   _____

ditch   _____

patch   _____

limb   _____

align   _____

wrench   _____

clutch   _____

snatch   _____

Lesson 5 Silent Letters: Words with **gn**, **mb**, **tch**, and **wr**

Words in Context
Write the missing spelling words.

Building a Birdhouse

> **Challenge**
>
> Circle the other words with
> **gn**, **mb**, **tch**, and **wr**.

Our art class had an interesting

assignment. We each had to _____ a birdhouse. I began by

making a _____. I didn't have a ruler, so I used the edge of

my _____ to draw straight lines. When I was finished, I began

to _____ the materials I needed to build my birdhouse.

I took some wood, nails, and my drawing out to a tree in my

backyard. Then, I had to _____ my saw, a hammer, and a

_____ all at once and carry them to the tree. There, I saw

my cat try to _____ my drawing. I knew that he was trying

to _____ my plan to build a safe place for birds. I chased

him into a _____ at the end of the yard. Then, I smoothed

out the _____ in my drawing. I carved a notch on a

_____ of the tree to mark the place for my birdhouse.

As I built it, I tried to _____ all the pieces of wood.

Now, a small brown _____ with a _____

of black on her throat often visits my birdhouse. She likes to watch my cat,

who can only stare back at her and _____ his whiskers. He

can't climb the tree.

Lesson 5 Silent Letters: Words with **gn**, **mb**, **tch**, and **wr**

Fun with Words

Write the spelling word that fits each sentence and has a consonant diagraph that sounds the same as the underlined letters.

1. Will you please _____ the ma<u>tch</u>es from the hu<u>tch</u>?

2. Rachel will i<u>r</u>on the _____ in he<u>r r</u>ed d<u>r</u>ess.

3. Can you _____ a si<u>gn</u> to sell bolo<u>gn</u>a?

4. The ca<u>tch</u>er tried to _____ the ball before it rolled into the di<u>tch</u>.

5. The _____ is the <u>wr</u>ong tool to use to <u>r</u>epai<u>r</u> the <u>r</u>ake.

6. Please _____ the twi<u>n</u>e with the stem of the vi<u>n</u>e.

7. Did you atta<u>ch</u> a _____ on your scra<u>tch</u>?

8. The tiny b<u>r</u>own _____ perched on the <u>wr</u>eath.

Words Across the Curriculum

Say each social studies word. Then, write the word.

1. wreath _____   3. lasagna _____

2. tomb _____   4. hitch _____

Write the social studies word that completes each sentence.

1. _____ is an Italian dish made with pasta, meat, and cheese.

2. Some people hang a _____ on the door during holidays.

3. Each pyramid in Egypt is the _____ of an ancient king or queen.

4. In the Old West, people used to _____ their horses to posts outside of stores.

Lesson 5 Silent Letters: Words with **gn**, **mb**, **tch**, and **wr**

Words in Writing

Write directions telling how to make or fix something. Use at least four words from the box.

_____

_____

_____

_____

_____

fetch	design	twitch	patch	wrench	wreath	tomb
wren	wreck	wrinkle	limb	clutch	lasagna	hitch
sketch	comb	ditch	align	snatch		

Dictionary Practice

Write the words from the box in alphabetical order. For some words, you will have to look at the third or fourth letter.

1. _____   8. _____   15. _____

2. _____   9. _____   16. _____

3. _____   10. _____   17. _____

4. _____   11. _____   18. _____

5. _____   12. _____   19. _____

6. _____   13. _____

7. _____   14. _____

Review Lessons 1–5

Write the spelling word that fits with each group of words.

1. lettuce, radish, carrot, _____

2. mattress, pillow, sheets, _____

3. peach, plum, apricot, _____

4. bolt, nut, nail, _____

5. rope, cord, twine, _____

6. sparrow, robin, finch, _____

7. milk, yogurt, butter, _____

8. soup, salad, chips, _____

9. brook, creek, stream, _____

10. hand, palm, thumb, _____

Write the spelling word that is a synonym for each word below.

11. shine   _____

12. propose   _____

13. excitement   _____

14. ruin   _____

15. flag   _____

16. end   _____

Review Lessons 1–5

Write the spelling word that means the same as each word below.

17. collect _____

18. shriek _____

19. toss _____

20. grab _____

21. branch _____

22. wriggle _____

Write the spelling word that completes each sentence.

23. Did you pack the food in the picnic _____?

24. The girls hung their coats in the _____.

25. The wheels of the old bike sound _____.

26. I taught my dog to _____ the newspaper.

27. I bought a _____ of ripe bananas.

28. Dad tightened the bolt on my bike with a _____.

29. I like the geometric _____ on that quilt.

30. Did you get _____ credit for your report?

Lesson 6 Words with the Long **a** Sound

Say each word. Listen for the long **a** sound. Then, write the word.

Spelling Tip	The long **a** sound can be spelled **a**, **a-consonant-e**, **ai**, **ay**, **ea**, and **eigh**. The symbol for the long **a** sound is /ā/.

Spelling Words

steak _____

plain _____

agent _____

weight _____

amaze _____

danger _____

brain _____

bacon _____

brave _____

escape _____

paper _____

neighbor _____

trace _____

cable _____

behave _____

Lesson 6 Words with the Long **a** Sound

Words in Context

Write the missing spelling words.

A Tall, Tall Tale

Challenge

Circle the other words with the /ā/ sound.

My dog Albert is incredible. The things he can do would truly _____ you. First of all, he uses his _____ to think like a human. He doesn't _____ like a dog at all. Albert likes to lay on the couch and watch cooking programs on _____ TV. He writes down the recipes on notebook _____. Last night, Albert invited our next-door _____ over for dinner. Albert made grilled _____, baked potatoes, and a salad topped with cheese and _____.

Albert is much more than a great cook. He is also a very _____ dog who tracks criminals in his spare time. He once helped a secret _____ catch an international thief. Albert trailed the thief along a beach in Maine. The thief thought that Albert was just a _____, ordinary dog. Thinking that he was in no _____ of being caught, the thief broke into a beach house and stole some jewels. He thought he would _____ from the house without leaving a _____ of evidence. But Albert threw all the _____ of his body at the thief and knocked him down. Then, he used his cell phone to call for backup.

Lesson 6 Words with the Long **a** Sound

Fun with Words

Write the spelling word that completes each comparison.

1. *Chalk* is to *board* as *pen* is to _____.

2. *Inches* is to *height* as *pounds* is to _____.

3. *Public* is to *police* as *secret* is to _____.

4. *Battery* is to *cell phone* as _____ is to *television.*

5. *Breathe* is to *lungs* as *think* is to _____.

6. *Steak* is to *potatoes* as _____ is to *eggs.*

7. *Amazing* is to *unusual* as *ordinary* is to _____.

8. *Afraid* is to *scared* as *fearless* is to _____.

9. *Thrill* is to *boredom* as *safety* is to _____.

10. *Unfriendly* is to *enemy* as *friendly* is to _____.

Words Across the Curriculum

Say each math word. Then, write the word.

1. scale _____   3. eighth _____

2. radius _____   4. table _____

Write the math word that fits each group of words.

1. row, column, data, _____

2. area, diameter, circumference, _____

3. fifth, sixth, seventh, _____

4. balance, spring, weigh, _____

Lesson 6 Words with the Long **a** Sound

Words in Writing

Write a tall tale using made-up characters and exaggeration. Use at least four words from the box.

_____

_____

_____

_____

_____

steak	weight	brain	escape	trace	scale	radius
plain	amaze	bacon	paper	cable	eighth	table
agent	danger	brave	neighbor	behave		

Dictionary Practice

Read the dictionary entries below. Then, read the example sentences. Write the part of speech and the number of the definition of the underlined words.

cable (kā´ bəl) *n.* **1.** a strong, thick cord. **2.** A bundle of wires enclosed in a protective covering and used to carry an electric current. *adj.* **1.** Transmitted by cable TV. *v.* **1.** To transmit a message.

plain (plān) *adj.* **1.** Clearly seen or heard. **2.** Obvious; clearly understood. **3.** Without decoration. **4.** ordinary. *n.* **1.** An area of level land.

1. The judge made it <u>plain</u> that he did not agree.   _____

2. Suspension bridges are held up by steel <u>cables</u>.   _____

3. The woman wore a <u>plain</u> black raincoat.   _____

4. I like to watch comedy shows on <u>cable</u> TV.   _____

Lesson 7 Words with the Long e Sound

Say each word. Listen for the long **e** sound. Then, write the word.

Spelling Tip	The long **e** sound can be spelled **e**, **ee**, **ea**, **ie**, **y**, and **ey**. The symbol for the long **e** sound is /ē/.

Spelling Words

steam   _____

sweet   _____

honey   _____

shield   _____

treat   _____

screech   _____

least   _____

beetle   _____

reason   _____

breathe   _____

field   _____

beast   _____

valley   _____

species   _____

monkey   _____

Lesson 7 Words with the Long **e** Sound

Words in Context

Write the missing spelling words.

Challenge

Circle the other words in the report with the /ē/ sound.

Life in a Rain Forest

Tropical rain forests are the most diverse ecosystems on Earth. More than half of all plant and animal _____ live in rain forests, which receive at _____ 50 inches of rain per year. Sometimes, the rain is so warm that water droplets rise back into the air in the form of _____. Rain forest trees give off oxygen that animals need to _____. The trees are often clustered around a sloping river _____.

Most rain forest trees have leafy branches that grow only at the top. These branches, called the canopy, _____ the forest floor from sunlight. From above, the canopy looks like a huge green _____.

All kinds of nuts and tropical fruits that are as _____ as _____ grow in the canopy. For this _____, most rain forest animals live in the canopy. There, it is common to see a _____ or two swinging from branch to branch as they _____ loudly at one another and search for fruit, nuts, or a special _____, such as a cricket or a plump _____. A strange _____, called a *sloth*, also lives in the canopy.

Lesson 7 Words with the Long **e** Sound

Fun with Words

Circle the word in each sentence that is contained in the underlined spelling word. There can be more than one possible answer.

1. The impish <u>monkey</u> hid the key to his cage.

2. Let's eat a cookie for a <u>treat</u>.

3. The air that we <u>breathe</u> contains oxygen.

4. One swarm of bees can produce a lot of <u>honey</u>.

5. The driver needs to take at <u>least</u> one more turn before he heads east.

6. A team of scientists designed a new <u>steam</u> engine.

7. The student had a good <u>reason</u> for being late.

8. A black <u>beetle</u> is nibbling on the beet.

9. We like to eat <u>sweet</u> berries.

10. At the end of the alley, you can see the distant <u>valley</u>.

Words Across the Curriculum

Say each math word. Then, write the word.

1. mean _____

2. degree _____

3. capacity _____

4. median _____

Write each math word next to its definition.

1. a unit used to measure temperature _____

2. the middle number in a group of numbers arranged from least to greatest _____

3. the amount of liquid that a container can hold _____

4. the average of a group of numbers _____

Lesson 7 Words with the Long e Sound

Words in Writing

Write a short report about a rain forest animal. Use at least four words from the box.

_____

_____

_____

_____

_____

steam	shield	least	breathe	valley	mean	degree
reason	treat	beetle	field	species	capacity	median
honey	screech	sweet	beast	monkey		

Misspelled Words

Read the paragraph. Circle the six misspelled words. Then, write the words correctly on the lines below.

Several different speces of monkeys live in tropical rain forests. Most rain forest monkeys are very social, like humans. They chatter with one another and screach loudly to warn other monkeys when a dangerous beest is nearby. Monkeys eat leaves, sweate fruits, flowers, seeds, and insects. A favorite treat of some monkeys is fresh honee or a plump beatle.

_____   _____   _____

_____   _____   _____

Lesson 8 Words with the Long i Sound

Say each word. Listen for the long **i** sound. Then, write the word.

Spelling Tip	The long **i** sound can be spelled **i**, **i-consonant-e**, **igh**, and **y**. The symbol for the long **i** sound is /ī/.

Spelling Words

price   _____

mild   _____

supply   _____

fight   _____

invite   _____

surprise   _____

private   _____

divide   _____

slight   _____

lightning   _____

quite   _____

bicycle   _____

decide   _____

library   _____

drive   _____

Lesson 8 Words with the Long i Sound

Words in Context

Write the missing spelling words.

It's a Party!

Dear Mike,

I'm writing to _____ you to a _____ party

for Casey. The party is next Saturday at Highland Park, which is right next to

the public _____. The weather

should be sunny and _____, with

only a _____ chance of rain and

_____. Kristi and I reserved the

_____ shelter near the pond. The party starts at five o'clock.

We will have a large _____ of food and soda. After we eat,

we can _____ into two teams and play baseball. I bought

_____ a few water balloons for a very low _____,

so we can also have a water-balloon _____. We can

_____ later what other games to play.

I hope you can come to the party. I think it will be really exciting! You

could ride your _____ to my house, and then my dad can

_____ us both to the park. Let me know soon.

Your friend,
Robbie

Lesson 8 Words with the Long i Sound

Fun with Words

Write the spelling word that completes each quote.

1. "Life is like riding a _____. You don't fall off unless you stop pedaling." –Claude Pepper

2. "When elephants _____, it is the grass that suffers." –African proverb

3. "If you must play, _____ upon three things at the start: the rules of the game, the stakes, and the quitting time." –Chinese proverb

4. "A wizard is never late, Frodo Baggins. Nor is he early. He will always _____ precisely when he means to." –Gandalf, from *The Lord of the Rings*

5. "_____ and rule, unite and lead." –Johann Wolfgang von Goethe

6. "When you reach for the stars you may not _____ get one, but you won't come up with a handful of mud either." –Leo Burnett

Words Across the Curriculum

Say each science word. Then, write the word.

1. tide _____
2. biome _____
3. hydrogen _____
4. vitamin _____

Write the science word that completes each sentence.

1. The Sun is made up of mostly helium and _____ .

2. A _____ is a chemical compound that human bodies need.

3. A _____ is the rise and fall of surface water in the ocean.

4. A desert is a _____ that receives very little rain.

Lesson 8 Words with the Long i Sound

Words in Writing

Write a letter to a friend. Use at least four words from the box.

_____

_____

_____

_____

_____

_____

_____

price	fight	private	lightning	decide	tide	biome
mild	invite	divide	quite	library	hydrogen	vitamin
supply	surprise	slight	bicycle	drive		

Dictionary Practice

Divide the words below into syllables using hyphens. Use a dictionary if you need help.

1. invite _____

2. biome _____

3. supply _____

4. divide _____

5. private _____

6. hydrogen _____

7. lightning _____

8. surprise _____

9. library _____

10. bicycle _____

Lesson 9 Words with the Long o Sound

Say each word. Listen for the long **o** sound. Then, write the word.

Spelling Tip	The long **o** sound can be spelled **o**, **o-consonant-e**, **oa**, **ough**, and **ow**. The symbol for the long **o** sound is /ō/.

Spelling Words

over   _____

broke   _____

motion   _____

below   _____

choke   _____

stolen   _____

noble   _____

moment   _____

swallow   _____

notice   _____

spoke   _____

croak   _____

propose   _____

hollow   _____

although   _____

Lesson 9 Words with the Long o Sound

Words in Context

Write the missing spelling words.

The Fox and the Crow

A black crow sat on a limb of a

_____ tree. He was holding a piece of

cheese in his beak. The crow did not _____

the cheese. Instead, he held it in his beak so that the fox

sitting _____ the tree would

_____ it. The fox stared up at the crow for

a _____. Then, he _____

the silence.

    "My, what a handsome and _____ bird you are," said

the sly fox. "Too bad your voice is just an ugly _____.

    The crow became very angry. _____ he tried to

_____ back his words, he couldn't remain quiet.

    "That's not true! I have a beautiful voice," the crow boasted.

    As soon as he _____, the cheese fell from his beak. With

a single quick _____, the fox grabbed the cheese. The crow

groaned in despair as he watched the fox dine on the

_____ cheese.

    "Thank you," said the fox, running his tongue _____ his

lips. "May I _____ a word of advice? Eating is more

important than pride."

Lesson 9 Words with the Long o Sound

Fun with Words

Clichés are common figures of speech that people use over and over again. Write the spelling word that completes each cliché.

1. This is the straw that _____ the camel's back.

2. There's no point crying _____ spilled milk.

3. I decided to go shopping on the spur of the _____.

4. I was so sad that I had to _____ back my tears.

5. The lion is a _____ beast that's known as the king of the jungle.

6. We couldn't understand her, because she _____ in riddles.

7. That insult was really hard to _____.

8. _____ the thief looks honest, he lies like a rug.

Words Across the Curriculum

Say each science word. Then, write the word.

1. motor _____   3. rotate _____

2. ocean _____   4. proton _____

Write the science word that completes each sentence.

1. It takes Earth 24 hours to _____ on its axis.

2. An electric _____ changes electricity into mechanical energy.

3. The Pacific is the largest _____ on Earth.

4. A _____ has a positive charge.

Lesson 9 Words with the Long o Sound

Words in Writing

A fable is a short story that teaches a lesson about life. It includes a sentence or two at the end that tells what the lesson is. Write an existing fable in your own words, or make up a new one. Use at least four words from the box.

_____

_____

_____

_____

over	below	noble	notice	propose	motor	ocean
broke	choke	moment	spoke	hollow	rotate	proton
motion	stolen	swallow	croak	although		

Misspelled Words

Read the first paragraph of the fable. Circle the five misspelled words. Then, write the words correctly on the lines below.

A town mouse invited his country cousin over for dinner. The two mice were enjoying the scraps left on the dining table from a noable feast. They didn't noetice the mosion of the hungry cat entering the room, although they did hear a most frightening noise: a sound like the purring of a motore. The two mice froze and looked into the darkness beloe the table.

_____   _____   _____

_____   _____

Lesson 10 Words with the Long **u** and /ü/ Sounds

Say each word. Listen for the long **u** and /ü/ sound. Then, write the word.

Spelling Tip	The long **u** sound can be spelled **o-consonant-e**, **u**, **ue**, **iew**, **u-consonant-e**. The symbol for the long **u** sound is /ū/. The **oo** sound can be spelled **ew**, **u-consonant-e**, **oo**, and **ue**. The symbol for the /oo/ sound is /ü/.

Spelling Words

proof _____

duty _____

stew _____

issue _____

review _____

smooth _____

value _____

whose _____

troop _____

truce _____

regular _____

include _____

argue _____

usually _____

continue _____

Lesson 10 Words with the Long **u** and /ü/ Sounds

Words in Context

Write the missing spelling words.

Please Join Our Group

Would you like to join a group of fun

people? If so, we would like to _____ you as a member of

our scouting _____. Our _____ meetings are

on the first Tuesday of each month.

At our meetings, we

_____ make plans for future

activities. We also collect dues, which we use to pay for our activities. We

_____ any other _____ that scout members

want to discuss. We try not to _____ about these matters or

lose our tempers. Instead, we talk calmly and try to _____

out any disagreements. We truly _____ every person's

opinion. If we can't agree on something, we call a _____.

Then, we _____ the discussion at the next meeting.

Our scouts have a strong sense of _____ to our

community. This year, we had a yard sale to raise money for a family

_____ house was damaged by a fire. We also made a

huge batch of beef _____ for the homeless center. These

activities are _____ of our commitment to our community.

Lesson 10   Words with the Long **u** and /ü/ Sounds

Fun with Words

Unscramble the letters to make spelling words. Then, unscramble the letters that you circle to solve the riddle.

1. grealru _____ Circle letter 5.

2. sweho _____ Circle letter 5.

3. dunlice _____ Circle letter 3.

4. wivere _____ Circle letter 4.

5. turfeu _____ Circle letter 6.

6. shomot _____ Circle letter 1.

7. notunice _____ Circle letter 3.

What is so fragile that even saying its name can break it? _____

Words Across the Curriculum

Say each art word. Then, write the word.

1. music _____   **3.** flute _____

2. unity _____   **4.** statue _____

Write the art word that fits with each group of words.

1. variety, harmony, balance, _____

2. piano, trumpet, guitar, _____

3. tune, melody, song, _____

4. painting, drawing, pottery, _____

Lesson 10 Words with the Long **u** and /ü/ Sounds

Words in Writing

Write a flyer that persuades people to join a club or other group. Use at least four words from the box.

_____

_____

_____

_____

_____

_____

_____

proof	issue	value	truce	argue	music	unity
duty	review	whose	regular	usually	flute	statue
stew	smooth	troop	include	continue		

Dictionary Practice

Write the number of syllables in each word below.

1. issue _____

2. unity _____

3. smooth _____

4. continue _____

5. duty _____

6. regular _____

7. statue _____

8. include _____

9. review _____

10. usually _____

Review Lessons 6-10

Write the spelling word that is an antonym of each word below.

1. safety _____

2. unite _____

3. solid _____

4. above _____

5. public _____

6. greatest _____

7. sour _____

8. rarely _____

9. fixed _____

10. rough _____

11. bought _____

Write the spelling word that belongs with each group of words.

12. juice, eggs, toast, _____

13. meadow, pasture, grassland, _____

14. skateboard, wagon, scooter, _____

15. string, cord, rope, _____

16. offer, suggest, advise, _____

Review Lessons 6-10

Write the spelling word that is a synonym of each word below.

17. simple _____

18. movement _____

19. evidence _____

20. protect _____

21. purpose _____

22. cost _____

23. very _____

24. battle _____

Write the spelling word that rhymes with each pair of words below.

25. beach, teach, _____

26. scoop, group, _____

27. lose, choose, _____

28. wake, break, _____

29. chunky, junky, _____

30. rally, tally, _____

31. dream, cream, _____

32. money, funny, _____

Lesson 11 Words with the /ôr/ Sound

Say each word. Listen for the /ôr/ sound. Then, write the word.

Spelling Tip	The /ôr/ sound can be spelled **or**, **ore**, and **our**.

Spelling Words

port   _____

force   _____

source   _____

support   _____

chore   _____

report   _____

before   _____

fort   _____

course   _____

order   _____

explore   _____

record   _____

border   _____

landform   _____

history   _____

Lesson 11 Words with the /ôr/ Sound

Words in Context

Write the missing spelling words.

A Famous Expedition

Challenge

Circle the other words in the report with the /ôr/ sound.

In 1804, Merriwether Lewis and William Clark began one of the most important journeys in American _____. By the _____ of President Thomas Jefferson, they left St. Louis to _____ the western United States. The year _____, the president had bought this territory from the French. The territory included the _____ city of New Orleans. It extended the western _____ of the United States from the Mississippi River to the Pacific Ocean.

Lewis and Clark began their journey aboard a keelboat on the Missouri River and followed the river to its _____. They took 50 men with them for protection and _____. They also built a _____. As the _____ of the river carried them along, Clark spent most of his time charting their _____ and making maps. He was very careful not to make an error in his calculations. Lewis's main _____ was to _____ his observations of the strange new animals, plants, and _____ that he saw. Lewis would later _____ this information to the president.

Lesson 11 Words with the /ôr/ Sound

Fun with Words

Use the letters of each spelling word below to make at least three four-letter words.

1. landform _____

2. course _____

3. support _____

4. record _____

5. before _____

6. history _____

7. Two of the spelling words have all of the same letters. The only difference is that two of the letters are reversed. Which words are they?

_____

Words Across the Curriculum

Say each social studies word. Then, write the word.

1. court _____   **3.** uniform _____

2. afford _____   **4.** export _____

Write the social studies word that completes each sentence.

1. The United States and Canada _____ many goods.

2. If you can't _____ to buy something you want right away, you can wait until you save enough money.

3. A trial is held in a _____.

4. A police officer wears a _____ so that people can identify him or her.

Lesson 11 Words with the /ôr/ Sound

Words in Writing

If you could live in any place at any time in history, where would it be? Write about this time and place. Use at least four words from the box.

_____

_____

_____

_____

_____

_____

port	support	before	order	border	court	afford
force	chore	fort	explore	landform	uniform	export
source	report	course	record	history		

Misspelled Words

Read the description. Circle the five misspelled words. Then, write the words correctly on the lines below.

　　If I could go back in history, I'd like to live about 100 years ago. I would live on a tropical island in the days befor many tourists visited it. I would explour every beach and landforme. I'd keep a journal to recorde all the interesting things I saw. I would also sail on a boat beyond the boreder of the land.

_____ _____ _____ _____

_____ _____

Spectrum Spelling
Grade 4

Lesson 11
Words with the /ôr/ Sound

53

Lesson 12 Words with the /ûr/ Sound

Say each word. Listen for the /ûr/ sound. Then, write the word.

Spelling Tip	The /ûr/ sound can be spelled **er**, **ear**, **ir**, **or**, and **ur**.

Spelling Words

curve   _____

heard   _____

worry   _____

further   _____

perfect   _____

worth   _____

return   _____

shirt   _____

hurry   _____

surge   _____

expert   _____

search   _____

purpose   _____

certain   _____

thirsty   _____

Lesson 12 Words with the /ûr/ Sound

Words in Context

Write the missing spelling words.

Earning a Comeback

This morning was my first soccer game of the season, but I overslept. I had to _____ through my closet for my gear and _____ to the field as quickly as I could. I was _____ that I'd be late, but it turned out that there was no need to _____. The game hadn't started yet.

I took off my _____ and put on my jersey. Then, I _____ the referee blow his whistle, so I joined my team on the field. During the first half of the game, the opposing team dominated us. Our players pursued the ball without any real _____. At halftime, we were discouraged, hot, and _____. We did not think it was _____ the effort to _____ to the field to face _____ embarrassment.

Somehow, our coach managed to encourage us. He is an _____ at making us focus on doing our best. We came back in the second half with a _____ of energy. With the score tied near the end of the game, our best striker scored a _____ goal. He faked around his defender and was able to _____ the ball into the top of the goal.

Lesson 12 Words with the /ûr/ Sound

Fun with Words

Use the clues to complete the puzzle with spelling words.

Across

1. look for
3. needing water
4. just right
5. be troubled about
6. master or specialist

Down

1. a burst
2. sure
4. reason

Words Across the Curriculum

Say each science word. Then, write the word.

1. germ _____

3. current _____

2. Earth _____

4. pearl _____

Write the science word that completes each sentence.

1. A _____ can flow deep beneath the surface of the ocean.

2. The moon revolves around _____.

3. A _____ can be seen only with a microscope.

4. A _____ is a gem formed inside of an oyster.

Lesson 12 Words with the /ûr/ Sound

Words in Writing

Describe a sports event that you watched or participated in. Use at least four words from the box.

_____

_____

_____

_____

curve	further	return	surge	purpose	germ	Earth
heard	perfect	shirt	expert	certain	current	pearl
worry	worth	hurry	search	thirsty		

Dictionary Practice

Circle the correct pronunciation for the words below. Use a dictionary if you need help.

1. pearl   perl   pûrl   pûr el

2. curve   cûrve   kûrv   kerv

3. perfect   pûrf´ ect   per´ fek   pûr´ fikt

4. further   fur´ thur   fûr´ thər   ferth´ er

5. thirsty   thûrs´ tī   thir´ stē   thûr´ ste

6. heard   herd   hûred   hûrd

7. surge   surg   cûrj   sûrj

Lesson 13 Words with the /ə/ Sound

Say each word. Listen for the /ə/ sound in the final syllable. Then, write the word.

Spelling Tip	The /ə/ sound can be spelled **a**, **e**, and **o**. The /ə/ sound is common in unstressed syllables.

Spelling Words

model   _____

royal   _____

cotton   _____

central   _____

custom   _____

flavor   _____

towel   _____

happen   _____

local   _____

lemon   _____

jewel   _____

capital   _____

travel   _____

normal   _____

natural   _____

Lesson 13 Words with the /ə/ Sound

Words in Context

Write the missing spelling words.

An Unusual Shopping Trip

If you ever _____ to _____ to Egypt, be

sure to visit the famous marketplace in the middle of Cairo, the

_____ city. The marketplace has many ancient walls and

buildings, including a _____ palace. This marketplace is

nothing like a _____ mall in the United States.

Inside the _____ part of the

marketplace, there is a maze of shops that sell

almost any item that you can imagine. You

can find an inexpensive _____

of a famous piece of Egyptian art or a copy of a valuable

_____. You also can find a carpet, _____, or

other piece of cloth made of fine wool or _____.

Outside the marketplace, many _____ farmers set up

stalls with fruits, vegetables, and other _____ products,

which they unload each day from their wagons. You can almost taste the

bitter _____ of a juicy _____ or an exotic

spice. It is a _____ in Egypt to bargain with the shopkeepers

over their prices.

Lesson 13 Words with the /ə/ Sound

Fun with Words

The letters in one or two words in each sentence can be rearranged to form a spelling word. Circle the words and then rearrange the letters to make the spelling word.

1. I will not sit on that cot! _____

2. The lunar spaceship landed on the moon at noon. _____

3. My dad lent his car to his barber. _____

4. Would you like a ripe, juicy melon? _____

5. Did you lay your gloves down or did you lose them? _____

6. We bought a lot of apples today. _____

7. The old man gave me some wise advice. _____

8. I did a sum while I lay on the cot. _____

Words Across the Curriculum

Say each science word. Then, write the word.

1. metal _____   3. carbon _____

2. organ _____   4. water _____

Write the science word that completes each sentence.

1. The _____ that pumps blood in the body is the heart.

2. _____ is a mixture of hydrogen and oxygen.

3. A _____ is usually a hard, solid, shiny substance.

4. _____ is an element found in the remains of all living things.

Lesson 13 Words with the /ə/ Sound

Words in Writing

Describe a tradition in your family.
Use at least four words from the box.

_____

_____

_____

_____

_____

_____

_____

model	central	towel	lemon	travel	metal	organ
royal	custom	happen	jewel	normal	carbon	water
cotton	capital	local	flavor	natural		

Misspelled Words

Read the description. Circle the five misspelled words. Then, write the words correctly on the lines below.

My grandmother is from the centrel part of Greece. She isn't able to traval there very often, but she still follows many Greek customs. She makes Greek food using naturel ingredients that she buys from a local farm market. She uses lemen juice to add a tart flaver to many of the dishes she makes.

_____   _____   _____

_____   _____

Review Lessons 11–13

Write the spelling word that is an antonym of each word below.

1. closer _____

2. after _____

3. unsure _____

4. game _____

5. unusual _____

6. leave _____

Write the spelling word that is a synonym of each word below.

7. goal _____

8. tradition _____

9. command _____

10. arch _____

11. taste _____

12. occur _____

13. mistake _____

14. edge _____

15. value _____

Review Lessons 11–13

Write the spelling word that belongs with each group of words.

16. mountain, desert, volcano, _____

17. aching, tired, hungry, _____

18. pants, sweater, vest, _____

19. king, queen, prince, _____

20. orange, grapefruit, lime, _____

21. velvet, wool, silk, _____

22. diamond, ruby, emerald, _____

23. seek, hunt, pursue, _____

24. journey, trip, visit, _____

25. robe, washcloth, sponge, _____

26. inform, notify, broadcast _____

27. origin, root, beginning, _____

28. pro, master, specialist _____

29. help, aid, assistance, _____

30. power, strength, might, _____

Lesson 14 Possessive Nouns

Say each word. Notice how the order of the **s** and the apostrophe shows whether the word is singular or plural. Then, write the word.

Spelling Tip	**Possessive nouns** are words that show ownership. When a noun shows that one person or thing owns something, the noun ends with **'s**. Usually, when a noun shows that more than one person or thing owns something, the noun ends with **s'**.

Spelling Words

baby's   _____

mother's   _____

brothers'   _____

officer's   _____

friend's   _____

sister's   _____

children's   _____

family's   _____

everyone's   _____

hamster's   _____

friends'   _____

father's   _____

grandmothers'   _____

customers'   _____

families'   _____

Lesson 14 Possessive Nouns

Words in Context

Write the missing spelling words.

Everything Not Being Used Must Go!

This summer, the people on my block had a big yard sale. The sale

was held in my _____ yard. This was my

_____ idea. At first, she just wanted to get rid of my

youngest _____ old dresses and coats. Then, she decided

that both of my _____ old baseball equipment had to go,

too. She began searching through _____ closets and

drawers to see what she could get rid of. She even went through my

_____ office to find things that he didn't use anymore.

My mother offered to help clear out some of her _____

houses, too. Soon, our yard was filled with other _____ old

and unused items. There was a _____ crib, a

_____ cage, an old police _____ uniform,

and all kinds of _____ toys and clothes. My best

_____ mother brought over a box full of both of her

_____ old-fashioned

dresses. When the sale was over, we

had collected more than $200 of our

_____ money.

Lesson 14 Possessive Nouns

Fun with Words

Write the spelling word that explains the relationship described in each sentence.

1. My mother's sons' bikes are my _____ bikes.

2. My parents' mothers' coats are my _____ coats.

3. My mother's daughter's desk is my _____ desk.

4. My grandfather's only son's car is my _____ car.

5. My buddy's mother is my _____ mother.

6. My aunt's only sister's dog is my _____ dog.

7. My parents' _____ toys are my brother's and sister's toys.

8. My parents' and their children's house is my _____ house.

Words Across the Curriculum

Say each art word. Then, write the word.

1. painters' _____

2. dancers' _____

3. actors' _____

4. artists' _____

Write the missing art words.

People enjoy many different kinds of _____ work. Some

people like to visit museums to see their favorite _____ works

of art. Some people enjoy going to a play to see the _____

performances. Others enjoy watching a group of _____

movements onstage.

Lesson 14 Possessive Nouns

Words in Writing

Write a short story about something funny or interesting that happened to you or members of your family. Use at least four words from the box.

_____

_____

_____

_____

_____

baby's	friend's	everyone's	families'	actors'
mother's	sister's	hamster's	grandmothers'	dancers'
brothers'	children's	friends'	customers'	artists'
officer's	family's	father's	painters'	

Misspelled Words

Read the story. Circle the four possessive nouns that are used or spelled incorrectly. Then, write the correct possessive nouns.

    I was taking care of my best friends' hamster while he went to his familys' cabin for a week. On the second morning, the hamsters' cage was empty. My oldest sister's cat was licking its paws in a corner of my room. I gasped and ran into my parents' bedroom. I couldn't understand why they were both laughing. Then, I saw the hamster curled up inside one of my fathers' slippers.

_____   _____

_____   _____

Lesson 15 Easily Misspelled Words

Say each word. Look for familiar and unfamiliar spelling patterns. Then, write the word.

Spelling Tip	Some words have unusual spellings. You have to remember how these words are spelled.

Spelling Words

person _____

sure _____

touch _____

tropical _____

young _____

island _____

built _____

against _____

different _____

palm _____

awhile _____

answer _____

mountain _____

remember _____

camera _____

Lesson 15 Easily Misspelled Words

Words in Context

Write the missing spelling words.

A Vacation in Paradise Awaits You

Would you like to relax for _____ on a quiet beach

without having another _____ in sight? If the

_____ to this question is yes, please plan to visit our beautiful

_____. You will be _____ to enjoy your stay.

You can lie in a hammock under a _____ tree as a cool

breeze blows gently _____ your skin. You can wade along

the shore and feel the warm _____ of the sparkling blue

ocean.

There are many _____ things to do here, whether you

are old or _____. You can hike up the stone steps that were

_____ into the slope of a _____ hundreds of

years ago. You also can take a walk through our _____ rain

forest. _____ to bring your _____ so you can

take pictures of the beautiful scenery.

Lesson 15 Easily Misspelled Words

Fun with Words

Alliteration is when a group of words have the same beginning sound. Use alliteration to write the spelling word that best fits each sentence.

1. She's _____ she saw sheep shivering in the shade.

2. Tourists tried to twist through the trails under the _____ trees.

3. Bill _____ a box with black and blue blocks.

4. You'll be _____ for years.

5. The members must _____ to meet at midnight.

6. Dino demands a _____ dish every day for dinner.

7. Ann acted _____ Aunt Alice's advice.

8. Ken's _____ captured a captivating shot of the calico cats.

9. We will wait _____ for warmer weather.

Words Across the Curriculum

Say each math word. Then, write the word.

1. height _____

3. cylinder _____

2. symbol _____

4. graph _____

Write the math word that completes each sentence.

1. A tube is shaped like a _____.

2. The volume of a rectangle is its length times its width times its

   _____.

3. Ordered pairs can be plotted on a _____.

4. The _____ for cubic centimeters is cm³.

Lesson 15 Easily Misspelled Words

Words in Writing

Write an ad for a vacation spot that you would like to visit. Use at least four words from the box.

_____

_____

_____

_____

_____

_____

_____

_____

person	tropical	built	palm	mountain	height	symbol
sure	young	against	awhile	remember	cylinder	graph
touch	island	different	answer	camera		

Dictionary Practice

Use hyphens to show where to divide each word into syllables. Use a dictionary if you need help.

1. camera _____

2. mountain _____

3. answer _____

4. cylinder _____

5. different _____

6. remember _____

7. measure _____

8. symbol _____

Lesson 16 Irregular Plurals

Say each pair of words. Notice how the spelling of the plural form is different from the singular form. Also notice that one word does not have a singular form. Then, write each plural word.

| Spelling Tip | When a noun ends with **f** or **fe**, change the **f** or **fe** to **v** before adding **es**. A few nouns have plural forms that you have to remember. |

Spelling Words

leaf	leaves	_____
calf	calves	_____
life	lives	_____
ox	oxen	_____
wife	wives	_____
half	halves	_____
mouse	mice	_____
wolf	wolves	_____
thief	thieves	_____
loaf	loaves	_____
goose	geese	_____
knife	knives	_____
shelf	shelves	_____
scarf	scarves	_____
themselves		_____

Lesson 16 Irregular Plurals

Words in Context

Write the missing spelling words.

The Story of Ali Baba

Challenge

Circle the other plural nouns in the story.

A popular Middle Eastern folktale tells the story of Ali Baba and the forty _____. Ali Baba found the robbers' secret cave hidden behind the _____ of some thick bushes. Ali Baba listened at the door of the cave. He knew that the robbers would attack him like a pack of _____ pouncing on a flock of _____ or a herd of helpless _____ if they found him there. He heard nothing but a few _____ nibbling on _____ of bread.

When Ali Baba entered the cave, he saw all kinds of treasures heaped upon _____ and tables. He saw piles of gold and valuable goods, such as ladies' _____ and sharp _____ with jeweled handles. Ali Baba loaded a few bags of treasure onto his _____.

Ali Baba and his brother Cassim got along well, but their _____ stirred up trouble. Cassim's wife thought that the brothers should split the treasure between _____ in two _____. Cassim went to the cave and took so much treasure that the robbers noticed it was missing. The _____ of the brothers were in danger.

Lesson 16 Irregular Plurals

Fun with Words

Write the spelling word that names things you might find in each place.

1. inside a
   library _____

2. in a kitchen
   drawer _____

3. on a
   branch _____

4. with
   cows _____

5. at a pond _____

6. with their
   husbands _____

7. around people's
   necks _____

8. in a
   bakery _____

9. in the
   mountains _____

10. in prison _____

Words Across the Curriculum

Say each pair of words. Notice how the spelling of the plural form is different from the singular form. Also notice that one word does not have a singular form. Then, write the plural word.

1. elf   elves _____

2. woman women _____

3. child   children _____

4. ourselves _____

Write the missing irregular plural nouns.

1. The _____ made sandcastles on the beach.

2. _____ are imaginary creatures who sometimes help humans.

3. We are going to the park by _____.

4. Only a few men and _____ are chosen to be astronauts.

Lesson 16 Irregular Plurals

Words in Writing
Write your own folktale or fable. Use at least four words from the box.

_____

_____

_____

_____

leaves	oxen	mice	loaves	shelves	elves	women
calves	wives	wolves	geese	scarves	children	ourselves
lives	halves	thieves	knives	themselves		

Misspelled Words
Read the fable. Circle the five misspelled words. Then, write the words correctly.

A group of mouses once roamed the kitchen of a farmhouse. They climbed up the shelfs and tables, eating crumbs from loafs of bread and pieces of cheese. When the master of the house bought a cat, they held a meeting among themselfs to see how they could outwit the cat.

"Let's tie a bell around the cat's neck," said a young mouse.

"That's easy to say," replied an older mouse. "But who among us will actually risk their lifes to become heroes?"

_____   _____   _____

_____   _____

Lesson 17 Words with the Final /əl/ Sound

Say each word. Listen to the final /əl/ sound. Then, write the word.

Spelling Tip	The /əl/ sound at the ends of words is often spelled **le**.

Spelling Words

settle   _____

angle   _____

title   _____

bubble   _____

trouble   _____

sparkle   _____

kettle   _____

simple   _____

scramble   _____

terrible   _____

puzzle   _____

scribble   _____

tremble   _____

double   _____

trickle   _____

Lesson 17 Words with the Final /əl/ Sound

Words in Context

Write the missing spelling words.

The First National Park

Challenge

Circle the other words in the story with the final /əl/ sound spelled **le**.

Before the 1870s, pioneers had

not yet begun to _____ in Idaho,

Wyoming, and Montana. However, explorers told

incredible stories of hot water that would

_____ from the ground like water boiling

from a _____ on a stove. Sometimes,

they said the ground seemed to rumble and _____. The hot

water would spurt straight out of the ground at a right

_____ and _____ in the sunlight. Then, it

would slow to a _____. Afraid that something

_____ might happen to them, the explorers would

_____ to safety. Still, they took time to _____

brief notes about the geysers. How geysers worked was a _____

to early explorers, but it is _____ to understand.

In 1872, explorers had very little _____ convincing Congress

to set aside this remarkable land which became the first national park. It

contains more than _____ the amount of all the other geysers

on Earth. The park's _____ is Yellowstone National Park.

Lesson 17 Words with the Final /əl/ Sound

Fun with Words

Clichés are familiar phrases that have been used over and over again. Write the spelling word that completes each cliché.

1. The truth is pure and _____.

2. This is a fine _____ of fish!

3. I need to _____ a score with you.

4. Her eyes _____ like diamonds.

5. I don't want to burst your _____, but . . .

6. I started to _____ like a leaf in the wind.

7. The money began to slowly _____ in.

8. The detective finally put together the pieces of the _____.

Words Across the Curriculum

Say each science word. Then, write the word.

1. ankle   _____   3. cycle   _____

2. muscle   _____   4. particle   _____

Write the science word that belongs with each group of words.

1. atom, molecule, _____

2. bone, tendon, _____

3. water, life, _____

4. knee, elbow, _____

Lesson 17 Words with the Final /əl/ Sound

Words in Writing

Write notes about some things that you know about water. Use at least four words from the box.

_____

_____

_____

_____

_____

settle	bubble	kettle	terrible	tremble	ankle	muscle
angle	trouble	simple	puzzle	double	cycle	particle
title	sparkle	scramble	scribble	trickle		

Misspelled Words

Read the notes about water. Circle the five misspelled words. Then, write the words correctly.

Water on Earth goes through a simple sycle.

There's more than doubele the amount of water in oceans than in lakes and rivers.

Particels of water from oceans rise and collect in clouds.

When rain falls to Earth, some water drops setle in puddles. Others trikle from tree branches down to the ground.

_____   _____   _____

_____   _____

Lesson 18 Homophones

Say each word. Notice the different spellings of the words that sound the same. Then, write each word.

Spelling Tip	**Homophones** are words that sound the same but have different spellings and meanings.

Spelling Words

close   _____

sight   _____

poor   _____

peek   _____

groan   _____

waste   _____

clothes   _____

miner   _____

pour   _____

site   _____

peak   _____

waist   _____

grown   _____

pore   _____

minor   _____

Lesson 18 Homophones

Words in Context
Write the missing spelling words.

San Francisco, 1849

I arrived in San Francisco in 1849 to become a

gold _____. I spent most of my

money to pay my fare on the ship, so now I was

_____. I didn't have a penny to _____. This, I

thought, was only a _____ problem. Soon, I'd be rich.

With the money I had left, I bought some food and work

_____ at a general store. I put them on and strapped my

belt around my _____. As I paid for my goods, the store

clerk described how the city had _____ in the past year. I

reached behind me to _____ the door of the store and

began a new chapter of my life.

I started down the dusty trail with the _____ of a

mountain _____ looming before me. After a few days, I

found a good _____ to look for gold. With a loud

_____, I dropped my heavy pack. Sweat dripped from every

_____ of my skin. As I sat down by the creek bed and began

to _____ water over my head, I saw something sparkling in the

mud. I closed my eyes before I dared to take another _____.

Lesson 18 Homophones

Fun with Words

Write the spelling word that completes each quote.

1. "It's not the man who has too little that is _____; it's the man who always wants more." –Unknown

2. "Today I have _____ taller from walking with the trees." –Karl Baker

3. "_____ not, want not." –Benjamin Franklin

4. "A person who is out of _____ is soon out of mind." –Unknown

5. "You can't judge a book by its cover or a man by his

   _____." –Unknown

6. "Happiness is a perfume which you cannot _____ on someone without getting some on yourself." –Ralph Waldo Emerson

Words Across the Curriculum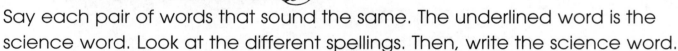

Say each pair of words that sound the same. The underlined word is the science word. Look at the different spellings. Then, write the science word.

1. <u>scent</u>, sent _____   3. foul, <u>fowl</u> _____

2. beat, <u>beet</u> _____   4. <u>heel</u>, he'll _____

Write the science homophone that completes each sentence.

1. A _____ is a vegetable that grows underground.

2. The rounded, back part of a human foot is the _____.

3. Ducks and geese are both water _____.

4. The color and _____ of a flower attracts bees.

Lesson 18 Homophones

Words in Writing

Make up some wise sayings, or proverbs.
Use at least four words from the box.

_____

_____

_____

close	peek	clothes	site	grown	scent	beet
sight	groan	miner	peak	pore	fowl	heel
poor	waste	pour	waist	minor		

Dictionary Practice

Read the dictionary entries. Then, write the part of speech and the number of the definition for the underlined word in each sentence.

waste *n.* **1.** The act of using carelessly. **2.** A wild or deserted place with few or no living things. *v.* **1.** To use up or spend in a careless way. **2.** To destroy or ruin.

foul *adj.* **1.** Unpleasant or disgusting. **2.** Very bad; evil. *v.* **1.** To make dirty. **2.** To break a rule in sports, especially by unfairly touching another player.

  1. The rotten bananas had a <u>foul</u> smell. _____

  2. The invading army <u>wasted</u> everything in its path. _____

  3. Watching that movie was a <u>waste</u> of time. _____

  4. I got a free throw because a player on the other team <u>fouled</u> me.

  _____

Review Lessons 14–18

Write the spelling word that is an antonym of each word.

1. same   _____

2. rich   _____

3. husbands   _____

4. wonderful   _____

5. forget   _____

6. old   _____

7. complex   _____

8. open   _____

9. question   _____

10. for   _____

Write the spelling word that belongs with each group of words.

11. eighths, fourths, thirds, _____

12. chicks, lambs, foals, _____

13. plates, forks, spoons, _____

14. hill, volcano, cliff, _____

15. point, line, side, _____

16. riddle, mystery, maze, _____

17. moan, shriek, cry, _____

18. twice, couple, pair, _____

Review Lessons 14–18

Write the spelling word that is a synonym of each word.

19. made _____

20. robbers _____

21. twinkle _____

22. dad's _____

23. shake _____

24. moms' _____

25. certain _____

26. name _____

Write the spelling word that completes each sentence.

27. The _____ crib was full of toys and blankets.

28. The autumn _____ are red and orange.

29. Are there many _____ trees on this island?

30. Mother likes to bake _____ of bread.

31. Do you have your _____ hat on?

32. _____ are members of the dog family.

Lesson 19 Words with the /j/ Sound

Say each word. Listen for the /j/ sound. Then, write each word.

Spelling Tip	The /j/ sound can be spelled **j**, **g**, or **dje**.

Spelling Words

bridge   _____

jazz   _____

image   _____

luggage   _____

jumble   _____

range   _____

message   _____

jockey   _____

manage   _____

gentle   _____

plunge   _____

cabbage   _____

lodge   _____

garbage   _____

dangerous   _____

Lesson 19 Words with the /j/ Sound

Words in Context

Write the missing spelling words.

What to Do?

Grown-ups always ask what I want to do when I grow up. There's such a large

_____ of things to do that I haven't decided yet. I'd like to be a _____,

but that would be very _____. Racehorses aren't known for being _____ animals. I'm afraid I'd fall off and _____ to the ground with my arms and legs all in a _____. I can just imagine the X-ray _____ of all the damaged bones in my body.

I wouldn't mind working in a ski _____. I could help the skiers take their _____ to their rooms and give them a _____ when someone wants to reach them. Or, I could work in the kitchen, chopping up _____ and other vegetables. I'd probably have to clean the whole kitchen and take out the _____, too. On second thought, if I worked in a ski resort, I'd want to _____ all the other workers. Or, I could be an engineer and design the longest _____ in the world. I could play in a _____ band at night.

Lesson 19 Words with the /j/ Sound

Fun with Words

Write the spelling word that answers each clue.

1. If you travel a lot, you have to lug me around.   _____

2. I come from ragtime and the blues.
   Bebop, rock, and hip-hop came from me.   _____

3. My job is racing, but I don't run.   _____

4. You see me when you look in a mirror.   _____

5. Nobody likes me; everyone always
   wants to get rid of me.   _____

6. I bring places together.   _____

7. I am the head of the garden.   _____

8. I shelter people in the woods and mountains.   _____

Words Across the Curriculum

Say each social studies word. Then, write the word.

1. jury   _____   3. badge   _____

2. gypsy   _____   4. justice   _____

Write the social studies word that completes each sentence.

1. A police officer wears a _____ to identify himself or herself.

2. The court system is meant to provide _____ for all citizens.

3. We heard singing and clapping coming from the _____ camp.

4. A judge or a _____ can make a decision in a legal trial.

Lesson 19 Words with the /j/ Sound

Words in Writing

Describe a trip that you'd like to take.
Use at least four words from the box.

_____

_____

_____

_____

_____

_____

bridge	luggage	message	gentle	dangerous	jury	gypsy
jazz	jumble	jockey	plunge	lodge	badge	justice
image	range	manage	cabbage	garbage		

Misspelled Words

Read the description. Circle the four misspelled words. Then, write the
words correctly.

I'd like to stay at a ski lodje in the mountains. As soon as I got there, I'd

take my luggadge to my room and put on my ski clothes. I'd leave a

messaje for my parents that I would be on the slopes all day. I'd get my ski

badge, ride the ski lift up a mountain, and plundge down the slope.

_____   _____

_____   _____

Lesson 20 Words with the /k/ Sound

Say each word. Listen for the /k/ sound. Then, write each word.

Spelling Tip	The /k/ sound can be spelled **c**, **k**, and **ck**.

Spelling Words

junk _____

socket _____

carpet _____

kangaroo _____

corner _____

picnic _____

ticket _____

candle _____

bucket _____

creaky _____

attack _____

plastic _____

racket _____

attic _____

hockey _____

Lesson 20 Words with the /k/ Sound

Words in Context

Write the missing spelling words.

Be Careful of Rainy Days

> **Challenge**
>
> Circle the other words in the story with the /k/ sound.

One rainy day last week, I decided to

explore the _____. Holding out a lit

_____ in front of me, I crept up the

_____ old stairs. They were barely

covered by a worn-out _____. I kept

looking back over my shoulder as if someone might

sneak up and _____ me from behind.

When I got to the top of the stairs, I looked around and saw all kinds

of _____. In one _____, there was a rusty

metal _____ next to a wicker _____ basket.

Next to these was a trunk filled with sports equipment, including a

_____ stick, ice skates, and a tennis _____.

Nearby, a stuffed _____ seemed to stare at me with one

_____ black eye. Scattered across an old desk were letters,

postcards, and even an old movie _____.

Suddenly, I heard footsteps behind me on the stairs. My mother

appeared and plugged a lamp into a _____. "I'm so glad

you're here to help me clean up this mess," she said with a wicked smile.

Lesson 20 Words with the /k/ Sound

Fun with Words

Write the spelling word that fits each comparison.

1. *Curtain* is to *window* as _____ is to *floor*.

2. *Soccer* is to *grass* as _____ is to *ice*.

3. *Basement* is to *bottom* as _____ is to *top*.

4. *Snake* is to *slither* as _____ is to *hop*.

5. *Bat* is to *baseball* as _____ is to *tennis*.

6. *Straw* is to *basket* as *metal* is to _____.

7. *Bulb* is to *flashlight* as *flame* is to _____.

8. *Curve* is to *circle* as _____ is to *square*.

9. *Hug* is to *friend* as _____ is to *enemy*.

10. *Lunchbox* is to *lunch* as *basket* is to _____.

Words Across the Curriculum

Say each science word. Then, write the word.

1. climate _____   3. volcano _____

2. cricket _____   4. compound _____

Write each science word next to its definition.

1. a substance made of two or more elements   _____

2. a hopping insect related to a grasshopper   _____

3. a mountain that ejects lava and hot rocks   _____

4. the weather patterns in an area   _____

Lesson 20 Words with the /k/ Sound

Words in Writing

Describe a place in your home where many things are stored. Use at least four words from the box.

_____

_____

_____

_____

_____

_____

_____

junk	kangaroo	ticket	creaky	racket	climate	volcano
socket	corner	candle	attack	attic	compound	cricket
carpet	picnic	bucket	plastic	hockey		

Dictionary Practice

Write four words from the box that have each sound listed below. You might use a word in more than one column.

Short a Sound

_____

_____

_____

_____

Short i Sound

_____

_____

_____

_____

Short o Sound

_____

_____

_____

_____

Lesson 21 Words with the /s/ Sound

Say each word. Listen for the /s/ sound. Then, write each word.

Spelling Tip	The /s/ sound can be spelled **c** or **s**.

Spelling Words

silent   _____

suit   _____

special   _____

sorry   _____

notice   _____

ceiling   _____

promise   _____

sudden   _____

cereal   _____

select   _____

circus   _____

office   _____

sentence   _____

balance   _____

celebrate   _____

Lesson 21 Words with the /s/ Sound

Words in Context
Write the missing spelling words.

Birthday Surprise

Last Saturday was my birthday. As I was eating my breakfast of _____ and juice, my dad came downstairs. He was dressed in a _____ and tie. He looked like he was ready to go to his _____ and work. He had forgotten his _____ to spend this _____ day with me.

My dad was very _____ that he had forgotten. He took me to the mall and let me _____ some games and CDs. Then, we went to the _____. We had a great time there. I especially enjoyed watching the acrobats _____ on the high wire.

When we got back home, our house was dark and _____. I didn't _____ anything unusual. All of a _____, the lights went on. The _____ was covered with floating balloons and a banner with a _____ that said, " Have a great year!" My friends were all there to _____ my birthday!

Lesson 21 Words with the /s/ Sound

Fun with Words

Solve the puzzle with spelling words.

Across

2. a set of clothes
4. words that express a complete thought
6. a vow or word of honor
7. breakfast food
8. fast and without warning

Down

1. see
3. a place to do paperwork
4. without sound
5. a traveling show

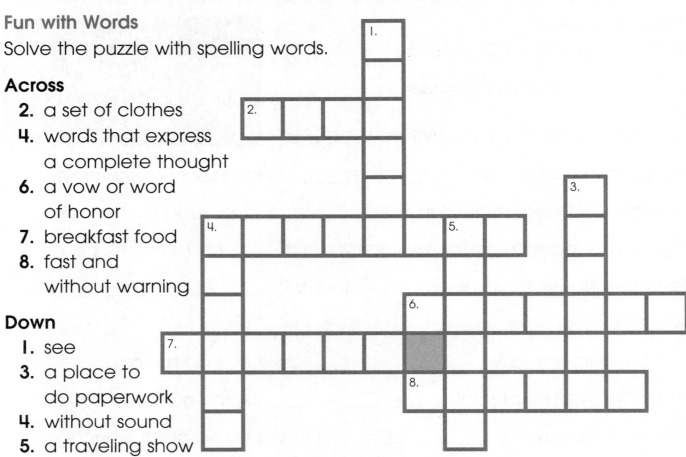

Words Across the Curriculum

Say each science word. Then, write the word.

1. solid _____   3. icicle _____

2. surface _____   4. science _____

Write each science word next to the pair of words it belongs with.

1. outside, top _____

2. frost, snow _____

3. math, art _____

4. gas, liquid _____

Lesson 21 Words with the /s/ Sound

Words in Writing

Write about a day that was important to you. Use at least four words from the box.

_____

_____

_____

_____

_____

_____

silent	sorry	promise	select	sentence	solid	surface
suit	notice	sudden	circus	balance	icicle	science
special	ceiling	cereal	office	celebrate		

Misspelled Words

Read the description. Circle the five misspelled words. Then, write the words correctly.

Last winter, there was a suddin snowstorm during the night. When I went outside the next morning, I noticed that everything was cilent and covered with snow. The surfase of our pond was frozen solud. My sister and I skated on the pond all day. I was sory when the day ended.

_____   _____   _____

_____   _____

Lesson 22 Words with **ex-**

Say each word. Look for familiar spelling patterns. Then, write each word.

Spelling Tip	The **ex-** spelling usually comes at the beginnings of words.

Spelling Words

except   _____

example   _____

exciting   _____

exactly   _____

extend   _____

expect   _____

excuse   _____

explain   _____

express   _____

exert   _____

exercise   _____

exhausted   _____

excellent   _____

expensive   _____

extremely   _____

Lesson 22 Words with **ex-**

Words in Context

Write the missing spelling words.

Challenge

Circle the other words in the essay with **ex**.

Why Not Try Tennis?

Playing tennis is an _____

way to _____ while playing a fun sport. The match I recently

played is a perfect _____. I didn't really

_____ the match to _____ any longer than

an hour. However, the match ended up taking _____ two

hours and twenty-two minutes. I had to _____ every extra

bit of energy I had to finish the match, but I still lost. I tried not to

_____ my disappointment about losing. Afterwards, my

opponent and I were both _____. We were moving

_____ slowly when we exited the tennis court.

Some people tell me that they don't play tennis because it's too

_____. I think that they just say this as an

_____ not to play. I _____ to them that once

they have a racket and tennis shoes, they don't have to spend any more

money _____ to buy new tennis balls once in a while. I also

tell them that you don't have to be an expert player to enjoy tennis. It's

an _____ game that everyone should try.

Lesson 22 Words with **ex-**

Fun with Words

Write the spelling word that fits each sentence and rhymes with the underlined word.

1. The police _____ to question the <u>suspect</u>.

2. Isn't it _____ that they're <u>inviting</u> us to the concert?

3. I'd like to _____ my joy for your <u>success</u>.

4. Please _____ why you continue to <u>complain</u>.

5. That <u>sample</u> is an _____ of sandy soil.

6. My mom didn't <u>refuse</u> to _____ me from school today.

7. This spray seems to be an _____ insect <u>repellant</u>.

8. I had to _____ my strongest effort to stay awake and <u>alert</u>.

Words Across the Curriculum

Say each science word. Then, write the word.

1. examine _____   3. exhibit _____

2. explode _____   4. experiment _____

Write the science word or words that complete each sentence.

1. A dinosaur _____ is on display at the museum.

2. It's important to _____ the results of an

   _____ before drawing a conclusion.

3. Some chemicals _____ when they come in contact with oxygen.

Lesson 22 Words with **ex-**

Words in Writing

Write a persuasive paragraph about a sport you enjoy. Use at least four words from the box.

_____

_____

_____

_____

_____

except	exactly	excuse	exert	excellent	examine	explode
example	extend	explain	exercise	expensive	exhibit	experiment
exciting	expect	express	exhausted	extremely		

Dictionary Practice

Write the words from the box in alphabetical order. You will have to look at the third or fourth letter of each word.

1. _____ 8. _____ 15. _____

2. _____ 9. _____ 16. _____

3. _____ 10. _____ 17. _____

4. _____ 11. _____ 18. _____

5. _____ 12. _____ 19. _____

6. _____ 13. _____

7. _____ 14. _____

Review Lessons 19–22

Write the spelling word that rhymes with each word.

1. confess _____

2. mumble _____

3. picket _____

4. boot _____

5. refuse _____

6. peeling _____

7. squeaky _____

8. complain _____

9. handle _____

10. has _____

11. sponge _____

12. jacket _____

13. inviting _____

14. bunk _____

15. pocket _____

Review Lessons 19–22

Write the spelling word that belongs with each pair of words.

16. baseball, soccer, _____

17. word, paragraph, _____

18. model, sample, _____

19. cabin, inn, _____

20. rug, mat, _____

21. basement, garage, _____

22. letter, note, _____

Write the spelling word that is a synonym of each word.

23. pail   _____

24. trash   _____

25. very   _____

26. unsafe   _____

27. quiet   _____

28. choose   _____

29. tired   _____

30. operate   _____

31. costly   _____

Lesson 23 Words with the Prefixes **in-**, **re-**, and **un-**

Say each word. Listen to the first syllable. Then, write each word.

Spelling Tip	The prefix **in-** can mean *not* or *in*. The prefix **re-** often means *again*. The prefix **un-** means *not*.

Spelling Words

remove _____

unfair _____

instant _____

regret _____

unable _____

instead _____

review _____

unaware _____

invent _____

repeat _____

unless _____

incorrect _____

retreat _____

refuse _____

incomplete _____

Lesson 23 Words with the Prefixes **in-**, **re-**, and **un-**

Words in Context

Write the missing spelling words.

Challenge

Circle the other words in the journal entry with the suffixes **in-**, **re-**, and **un-**.

Going Fishing

On Saturday morning, my mom

made me _____ my latest math exam. I

had seven _____ answers, and one

problem was _____ because I hadn't

had time to finish it. I had to _____ all of

my calculations. The _____ I finished, my

best friend called and invited me to go fishing with him.

I was _____ that my dad had other plans for me. He

told me to clean my room _____ of going fishing. I thought

it was _____ of him to interrupt my plans, but I couldn't

_____ to clean my room. I was _____ to

_____ any excuses, but I did _____ all those

times when I left my clothes lying on the floor.

I was forced to _____ into my messy bedroom.

_____ I could clean it up quickly, I would have to forget

about fishing. For the next half-hour, I worked incredibly hard to

_____ every piece of trash and dirty clothing from my room.

Finally, I was free to go fishing.

Lesson 23 Words with the Prefixes **in**-, **re**-, and **un**-

Fun with Words

Write the spelling word that belongs to the same word family as each pair of words.

1. fairness, fairly, _____

2. correction, correctly, _____

3. preview, viewer, _____

4. ability, disabled, _____

5. completely, uncompleted, _____

6. inventor, invention, _____

7. unmoved, removal, _____

8. repetition, repeating, _____

9. refusal, refusing, _____

10. aware, awareness, _____

Words Across the Curriculum

Say each science word. Then, write the word.

1. recycle _____

2. instinct _____

3. unearth _____

4. react _____

Write the science word that completes each sentence.

1. Some metals _____ to oxygen by rusting.

2. Scientists _____ dinosaur bones very carefully.

3. You can _____ glass, paper, and plastic.

4. An _____ is a behavior that an animal is born knowing.

Lesson 23 Words with the Prefixes **in-**, **re-**, and **un-**

Words in Writing

Write a paragraph about something you cannot
do very well. Use at least four words from the box.

_____

_____

_____

_____

_____

remove	unable	invent	retreat	unearth
unfair	instead	repeat	refuse	instinct
instant	review	unless	incomplete	react
regret	unaware	incorrect	recycle	

Misspelled Words

Read the paragraph. Circle the five misspelled words. Then, write the
words correctly.

    I have to admit that I'm completely unabel to play basketball. I tried it
once, and it's an experience that I'll never repeet unless I grow about three
feet. Insted of getting the ball through the hoop, I could barely throw it over my
head. Still, my older brothers wouldn't let me reatreat from the court. I think
they had an unfaire advantage because they were much taller than I was.

_____   _____   _____

_____   _____

Lesson 24 Words with the Prefixes **dis-** and **mis-**

Say each word. Listen to the first syllable. Then, write each word.

Spelling Tip	The prefix **dis-** often means *the opposite of*. The prefix **mis-** often means *wrong* or *a lack of*.

Spelling Words

dislike   _____

mistake   _____

disturb   _____

dismiss   _____

misery   _____

dishonest   _____

disease   _____

misplaced   _____

discuss   _____

disappoint   _____

disagree   _____

misfortune   _____

discover   _____

disappear   _____

distribute   _____

Lesson 24 | Words with the Prefixes **dis**- and **mis**-

Words in Context

Write the missing spelling words.

A Surprising Discovery

When I _____ the

newspapers to my customers, I try to

_____ from sight as soon as I

deliver the paper to the last house. I don't want

to _____ the old man who lives

there. I don't _____ him, but some neighbors have told me

that he likes to argue and _____ with everyone.

Today, the old man was sitting on his porch. Much to my dismay, he asked

me to read the paper to him, because he had _____ his reading

glasses. He looked so distressed that I didn't want to _____

him, and I just couldn't make up a _____ excuse. Besides, I

felt sorry for him. I knew that he had the _____ of having a

_____ that kept him in constant _____.

I dismounted my bike and sat on the porch while reading the paper

to the old man. Then, he wanted to _____ the news before

he would _____ me from his porch. It didn't take me long to

_____ that I had made a _____ in judging

the old man. He isn't disagreeable at all.

Lesson 24 Words with the Prefixes **dis**- and **mis**-

Fun with Words

Write the spelling word that belongs to the same word family as each word below.

1. placement   _____

2. likely   _____

3. agreement   _____

4. easily   _____

5. fortunately   _____

6. appointment   _____

7. mission   _____

8. covering   _____

Words Across the Curriculum

Say each language arts word. Then, write the word.

1. misprint   _____

3. misspelled _____

2. misquote   _____

4. display   _____

Write the missing language arts words.

A newspaper editor has to make sure that a reporter doesn't

_____ a person who gives information. The editor edits

articles to correct any _____ words and tries to avoid any

kind of _____ in the paper. The editor also chooses photos

to _____ with the articles.

Lesson 24 Words with the Prefixes **dis-** and **mis-**

Words in Writing

Write directions that tell how you would research and write a newspaper article. Use at least four words from the box.

_____

_____

_____

_____

_____

_____

_____

_____

dislike	misery	discuss	discover	misspelled
mistake	dishonest	disappoint	disappear	misquote
disturb	disease	disagree	distribute	display
dismiss	misplaced	misfortune	misprint	

Dictionary Practice

Write *noun, verb,* or *adjective* to tell what part of speech each word is.

1. discover _____

2. misery _____

3. dishonest_____

4. disease _____

5. disturb _____

6. misfortune _____

7. disagree _____

8. disappear _____

Lesson 25 Words with the Suffix -ly

Say each word. Listen to the last syllable. Then, write each word.

Spelling Tip	Many adverbs end with **ly**.

Spelling Words

lonely _____

wisely _____

barely _____

rapidly _____

finally _____

truly _____

secretly _____

closely _____

eagerly _____

safely _____

totally _____

freely _____

perfectly _____

certainly _____

personally _____

Lesson 25 Words with the Suffix -ly

Words in Context

Write the missing spelling words.

Born Free

Challenge

Circle the other words in the story that end with the suffix **-ly**.

My dad was resting in his hammock so

comfortably that he was _____

awake. A _____ beautiful

butterfly with _____

matched markings on its wings fluttered by

him so _____ that I hardly

saw it. My dad suddenly became alert

and _____ watched the butterfly as it landed on a nearby

flower. I _____ don't know anything about butterflies, but

my dad does. He _____ crept towards it with a net, and I

_____ remained _____ silent.

_____, I hoped that my dad wouldn't catch the butterfly. I

thought it belonged in the garden, moving _____ from

flower to flower. If my dad kept it inside a terrarium, it would

_____ be very _____ all by itself.

_____, my dad had his net just above the butterfly

when our dog suddenly ran over to him and began barking loudly. Just in

time, the butterfly flew _____ away from the net.

Lesson 25 Words with the Suffix -ly

Fun with Words

Unscramble the underlined words to make spelling words. If there is more than one word underlined, combine both words, then unscramble them.

1. A <u>gray</u> <u>eel</u> slithered through the water.   _____

2. The <u>tall</u> boy got a new <u>toy</u> for his birthday.   _____

3. Did you see the gull <u>fly</u> over the <u>sea</u>?   _____

4. The children began to <u>cry</u> when they
   saw the <u>sleet</u> outside.   _____

5. We worked <u>nicely</u> together on our <u>art</u> projects.   _____

6. That <u>lady</u> has a <u>rip</u> in her coat.   _____

7. The soup is made of beef and <u>barley</u>.   _____

8. The farmer <u>nearly</u> slipped when
   he fed the <u>slop</u> to the pigs.   _____

Words Across the Curriculum

Say each social studies word. Then, write the word.

1. recently _____   3. daily _____

2. monthly _____   4. weekly _____

Write each social studies word next to its meaning.

1. every day   _____

2. not long ago   _____

3. once every seven days   _____

4. once every 28 to 31 days   _____

Lesson 25 Words with the Suffix -ly

Words in Writing

Write a newspaper article that describes a weather event. Use at least four words from the box.

_____

_____

_____

_____

_____

_____

lonely	rapidly	secretly	safely	perfectly	recently	monthly
wisely	finally	closely	totally	certainly	daily	weekly
barely	truly	eagerly	freely	personally		

Misspelled Words

Read the article. Circle the five misspelled words. Then, write the words correctly.

   A sudden storm swept rapidlly though the city today. Some people egerly reported that they bearly got safely inside their houses before the storm hit. Others said that they personaly saw a funnel cloud developing. They wisly took shelter in the basements of their homes.

_____   _____   _____

_____   _____

Lesson 26 Words with the Suffixes -ful and -less

Say each word. Listen to the last syllable. Then, write each word.

Spelling Tip	The suffix -**ful** means *full of*. The suffix -**less** means *without*.

Spelling Words

cheerful   _____

colorful   _____

spotless   _____

thankful   _____

graceful   _____

harmless   _____

hopeful   _____

restless   _____

wonderful   _____

frightful   _____

breathless   _____

thoughtful   _____

faithful   _____

motionless   _____

beautiful   _____

Lesson 26 Words with the Suffixes -ful and -less

Words in Context

Write the missing spelling words.

Thanks for the Memories

Dear Ms. Johnson,

I'm very _____ to you for the _____

time I had at your camp. I didn't see any _____ spiders;

the cabin was so clean that it was truly _____. The

_____ blend of blues and yellows inside the cabin always

made me feel _____. Also, the view of the peaceful

meadow was _____.

Whenever I got _____ from being inside the cabin, I found

many things to do outside. I enjoyed observing the _____

deer running through the woods. Although I was _____ with

excitement to be so close to them, I was careful to remain

_____ so they would know that I was _____.

I also want to let you know how grateful I am to your camp workers for

being so helpful and _____. I am _____ that I

will be able to return to your camp next year. I

will always be a _____ customer.

Sincerely,
Frankie Martinez

Lesson 26 Words with the Suffixes -ful and -less

Fun with Words

Write the spelling word that fits each description.

1. A runner after a race _____

2. A rainbow in the sky _____

3. A scary costume _____

4. A person making a wish _____

5. A room that's just been cleaned _____

6. A bike that no one is riding _____

7. A happy person _____

8. A bee that doesn't sting _____

9. A dog that loves its owner _____

10. A student writing a report _____

Words Across the Curriculum

Say each social studies word. Then, write the word.

1. careless _____   3. worthless _____

2. eventful _____   4. respectful _____

Write the social studies word next to its meaning.

1. without value _____

2. full of courtesy _____

3. full of things to see and do _____

4. without caution or attention _____

Lesson 26 Words with the Suffixes -**ful** and -**less**

Words in Writing

Write a letter thanking someone for something they did for you. Use at least four words from the box.

_____

_____

_____

_____

_____

_____

_____

_____

cheerful	graceful	wonderful	faithful	worthless
colorful	harmless	frightful	motionless	eventful
spotless	hopeful	breathless	beautiful	respectful
thankful	restless	thoughtful	careless	

Dictionary Practice

Write the root word of each spelling word below.

1. colorful _____

2. graceful _____

3. breathless _____

4. thoughtful _____

5. wonderful _____

6. harmless _____

7. thankful _____

8. beautiful _____

Review Lessons 23-26

Write the spelling word that is an antonym of each word.

1. ungrateful _____

2. dangerous _____

3. happiness _____

4. truthful _____

5. slowly _____

6. openly _____

7. ugly _____

8. clumsy _____

9. foolishly _____

10. alert _____

Write the spelling word that completes each sentence.

11. I can't leave _____ I ask my dad.

12. My brother looks _____ in his skeleton costume.

13. The frog hopped away the _____ I let go of it.

14. Sydney _____ her book and searched the whole house for it.

15. We have to _____ our muddy shoes before we go inside.

Review Lessons 23-26

Write the spelling word that is a synonym of each word.

16. wrong _____

17. illness _____

18. surely _____

19. completely _____

20. loyal _____

21. create _____

22. unmoving _____

23. find _____

24. error _____

25. unluckiness _____

26. honestly _____

27. happy _____

28. redo _____

29. lastly _____

30. bother _____

Lesson 27   Number Words

Say each word. Look for familiar spelling patterns. Then, write each word.

Spelling Tip	Many number words have familiar spelling patterns.

Spelling Words

thirty   _____

sixteen   _____

eleven   _____

billion   _____

forty   _____

thirteen   _____

fifteen   _____

eighteen   _____

fifty   _____

fourteen   _____

million   _____

nineteen   _____

twenty   _____

seventeen   _____

twelve   _____

Lesson 27 Number Words

Words in Writing

Write the missing spelling words.

Challenge

Circle the other words that name numbers or specific amounts.

Numbers

Numbers can be added and described in all kinds of ways. For example, _____ eggs or doughnuts make a dozen. Two quarters equal _____ cents, three dimes equal _____ cents, and three nickels equal _____ cents. Two weeks include _____ days, and two baseball teams have _____ players on the field at one time.

Two spiders together have _____ legs. Ten squares have _____ angles, while three triangles plus two squares have _____ angles. One less than a dozen is _____, and one more is _____. Two times ten is _____, and one less than that is _____.

Very large numbers describe some other things. Coal and oil formed more than a _____ years ago. There are more than a _____ stars in our galaxy.

Lesson 27 Number Words

Fun with Words

Solve each math problem with a numeral that represents a spelling word. Then, write the spelling word.

1. 10 + 7 = _____   _____

2. 100 – 50 = _____   _____

3. 32 ÷ 2 = _____   _____

4. 6 x 5 = _____   _____

5. 77 ÷ 7 = _____   _____

6. 5 x 8 = _____   _____

7. 40 –28 = _____   _____

8. 90 ÷ 6 = _____   _____

9. 39 ÷ 3 = _____   _____

10. 10 x 2 = _____   _____

Words Across the Curriculum

Say each math word. Then, write the word.

1. numeral _____   3. decimal _____

2. product _____   4. fraction _____

Write the word or words that complete each sentence.

1. A _____ is a part of a whole that can also be

   represented as a _____.

2. Any number can be spelled out or written as a _____.

3. A _____ results from multiplying two or more numbers.

Lesson 27 Number Words

Words in Writing

Write a paragraph describing what you might be doing at different ages in your life. Use at least four words from the box.

_____

_____

_____

_____

_____

_____

thirty	billion	fifteen	fourteen	twenty	numeral	product
sixteen	forty	eighteen	million	seventeen	decimal	fraction
eleven	thirteen	fifty	nineteen	twelve		

Misspelled Words

Read the paragraph. Circle the five misspelled words. Then, write the words correctly.

Right now, I'm elevin years old. When I turn forteen, I'll be a teenager. I will be glad to get my diver's license when I'm sixteen. When I'm eigtteen, I'll be able to vote. Maybe I'll make a millon dollars by the time I'm thirtey.

_____   _____   _____

_____   _____

Lesson 28 Words That End with -tion, -ture, and -ure

Say each word. Listen to the last syllable. Then, write each word.

Spelling Tip	The /shən/ sound is often spelled **tion**. The /chər/ sound is often spelled **ture**. The /yər/ sound is often spelled **ure**.

Spelling Words

nation   _____

moisture   _____

direction   _____

figure   _____

mention   _____

creature   _____

vacation   _____

pleasure   _____

condition   _____

location   _____

feature   _____

attention   _____

adventure   _____

protection   _____

furniture   _____

Lesson 28 Words That End with -tion, -ture, and -ure

Words in Context

Write the missing spelling words.

Dream House

Are you looking for the perfect

_____ home for you and your family? We have a house for

sale in a wonderful _____ on the beach. The house is the

creation of a famous builder. It's in excellent _____, and some

of the _____ and pictures inside will be sold with the house.

There's a huge deck that faces in the _____ of the ocean.

It's a real _____ to sit so close to the shore that you can feel

the _____ from the waves on your skin.

Another great _____ of the house is that it's next to one

of the most secluded nature preserves in the _____. You're

sure to have an interesting _____ every time you visit it. It's

common for an unusual _____ moving in the preserve to

catch the _____ of a person walking near it. The motion is

often caused by an unusual _____ that is under the

_____ of the government.

Please call us and _____ this ad. Hurry! This treasure will

be gone in the very near future.

Lesson 28 Words That End with -tion, -ture, and -ure

Fun with Words

Write the two spelling words that fit each sentence and have the same ending as the underlined word.

1. Please turn your _____ to the _____ of the <u>motion</u> picture on the screen.

2. It's always great to have an _____ surrounded by <u>nature</u>.

3. Did you <u>mention</u> the _____ of your favorite place to take a _____?

4. I hope there won't be any _____ on the patio _____ in the <u>future</u>.

5. The shadowy form of a mysterious _____ appeared in the <u>pasture</u>.

Words Across the Curriculum

Say each science word. Then, write the word.

1. caution _____   3. solution _____

2. measure_____   4. temperature_____

Write the science word or words that complete each sentence.

1. Ocean water is a common _____ made of salt and water.

2. You can _____ the _____ of an object in degrees Fahrenheit or Celsius.

3. Always use _____ when working with chemicals.

Lesson 28 Words That End with -**tion**, -**ture**, and -**ure**

Words in Writing

Write an ad that you could use to convince people to buy something that you own. Use at least four words from the box.

_____

_____

_____

_____

_____

_____

_____

nation	mention	condition	adventure	solution
moisture	creature	location	protection	measure
direction	vacation	feature	furniture	temperature
figure	pleasure	attention	caution	

Dictionary Practice

Write the root word of each word below. Use a dictionary if you need help.

1. location _____

2. moisture _____

3. direction _____

4. pleasure _____

5. protection _____

6. vacation _____

7. attention _____

8. adventure _____

Lesson 29 Adjectives That End with -**er** and -**est**

Say each word. Listen to the second syllable and the third syllable, if there is one. Then, write each word.

Spelling Tip	For adjectives that end with **y**, change the **y** to **i** before adding **er** or **est**.

Spelling Words

happy _____

cloudy _____

uglier _____

heaviest _____

pretty _____

happier _____

cloudiest _____

ugly _____

heavier _____

happiest _____

prettier _____

ugliest _____

heavy _____

cloudier _____

prettiest _____

Lesson 29 Adjectives That End with -er and -est

Words in Context

Write the missing spelling words.

An Unkind Princess

There once was a princess who was never

_____ than when she was playing with her golden balls. One

_____ day, the princess took three balls that she thought were

_____ than the others into the garden. Although they were

_____, the princess liked to toss them into the air. The

princess thought they were the _____ sight she had ever seen.

As she played, the _____ of the balls rolled into a deep well.

The princess was not _____ about this, and she began to cry.

Soon, an _____ frog poked his head out of the water.

"I'll get the ball if I can eat lunch with you at your dining table," said

the frog. Then, I'll be the _____ creature in the world instead

of the _____."

The princess's face became _____ than the sky as she

imagined the frog at her father's fine table. The frog seemed

_____ to her than ever. Still, the sky was the

_____ that she had ever seen. The princess couldn't go

inside without her _____ golden ball. Her heart felt

_____ every minute.

Lesson 29 Adjectives That End with -**er** and -**est**

Fun with Words

Unscramble the underlined words to make spelling words. If there is more than one word underlined, combine both words, then unscramble them.

1. As I began to eat my <u>rice</u>, I heard a <u>loud</u> noise. _____

2. Be careful not to <u>trip</u> on the rocks under the <u>tree</u>. _____

3. Let's <u>eat</u> the honey from the bee's <u>hives</u>. _____

4. I made a small <u>ship</u> out of paper and <u>tape</u>. _____

5. When my <u>pet</u> mouse gets tired,
   <u>it</u> likes to <u>rest</u> on my lap. _____

6. Mother took the pie <u>out</u> of the oven
   and <u>sliced</u> it into pieces. _____

Words Across the Curriculum

Say each science word. Then, write the word.

1. sunnier _____

2. sunniest _____

3. healthier _____

4. healthiest _____

Write the missing science words.

The _____ plants get just the right amount of sunlight

and water. Some plants need to be grown in _____

locations than other plants. A plant that needs constant light might need

to be moved to the _____ spot you can find. The plant will

soon become _____.

Lesson 29 Adjectives That End with -**er** and -**est**

Words in Writing

Write an ending to the story about the princess
and the frog. Use at least four words from the box.

_____

_____

_____

_____

_____

_____

happy	heaviest	cloudiest	happiest	heavy	sunnier	sunniest
cloudy	pretty	ugly	prettier	cloudier	healthier	healthiest
uglier	happier	heavier	ugliest	prettiest		

Misspelled Words

Read the ending to the story. Circle the four misspelled words. Then, write
the words correctly.

　　　The king was not happi with his daughter for trying to break her promise
to the frog. He told her that her actions were much ugleir than the way the
poor frog looked to her. He ordered the princess to find the frog as soon as
the cloudy sky became sunnyier. The princess was sorry that she had been
so cruel to the frog. When she found him, she felt much happyier.

_____ 　　　_____

_____ 　　　_____

Lesson 30 More Easily Misspelled Words

Say each word. Look for familiar and unfamiliar spelling patterns. Then, write the word.

Spelling Tip	Some words have unusual spellings. You have to remember how these words are spelled.

Spelling Words

believe _____

guess _____

century _____

machine _____

library _____

probably _____

recognize _____

separate _____

question _____

portrait _____

citizen _____

enough _____

government _____

biography _____

especially _____

Lesson 30 More Easily Misspelled Words

Words in Context

Write the missing spelling words.

Time for Research

For social studies class, I had to read

a _____ about a person

whose work I _____ was

_____ important to my

daily life. I didn't have

_____ information at home,

so I went to the _____ to do some research. I wanted a

quiet place to work, so I found a desk that was _____ from

the main research area.

I wasn't sure whether I wanted to read about a person who invented

an important _____ or a person who helped form the

_____ of our country. I was gazing around the room when I

saw a _____ of a person I didn't _____. My

_____ was that it was _____ a famous

_____ from the eighteenth _____. My

_____ was soon answered. The plaque under the painting

identified the person as the founder of the city.

Lesson 30 More Easily Misspelled Words

Fun with Words

Write the spelling word that completes each analogy.

1. <u>Command</u> is to <u>order</u> as _____ is to <u>ask</u>.

2. <u>Member</u> is to <u>club</u> as _____ is to <u>country</u>.

3. <u>Theater</u> is to <u>movie</u> as _____ is to <u>book</u>.

4. <u>Statue</u> is to <u>sculpture</u> as _____ is to <u>painting</u>.

5. <u>Combine</u> is to <u>unite</u> as _____ is to <u>divide</u>.

6. <u>Hammer</u> is to <u>tool</u> as <u>car</u> is to _____.

7. <u>Fact</u> is to <u>know</u> as <u>faith</u> is to _____.

8. <u>Ten</u> is to <u>decade</u> as one <u>hundred</u> is to _____.

9. <u>Surely</u> is to <u>certainly</u> as <u>possibly</u> is to _____.

Words Across the Curriculum

Say each science word. Then, write the word.

1. weather _____

2. equator _____

3. dinosaur _____

4. stomach _____

Write the missing science words.

1. The _____ separates the northern and southern hemispheres.

2. A _____ skeleton contains hundreds of bones.

3. Different climates on Earth experience different types of

   _____.

4. A female kangaroo has a pouch on her _____ for carrying babies.

Lesson 30 More Easily Misspelled Words

Words in Writing

Write a paragraph about an important American citizen. Use at least four words from the box.

_____

_____

_____

_____

believe	machine	recognize	portrait	biography	weather	equator
guess	library	separate	citizen	especially	dinosaur	stomach
century	probably	question	enough	government		

Dictionary Practice

Write the spelling words that fit in each column below. Some words belong in more than one column.

/e/ Sound	Long e Sound	Long i Sound
_____	_____	_____
_____	_____	_____
_____	_____	_____
_____	_____	_____
_____	_____	
_____	_____	
	_____	

Lesson 31 Compound Words

Say each word. Look for the two smaller words in each compound word. Then, write the word.

Spelling Tip	Many compound words are made of smaller words with familiar spelling patterns.

Spelling Words

highway _____

football _____

classmate _____

skateboard _____

motorcycle _____

newspaper _____

background _____

notebook _____

stoplight _____

sideline _____

crosswalk _____

somewhere _____

grandstand _____

brainstorm _____

scrapbook _____

Lesson 31 Compound Words

Words in Context

Write the missing spelling words.

At the Park

Sometimes, I walk to the park near my home in the afternoon. I turn left at the second _____ and then follow the _____ into the park. Usually, I walk by myself along the _____ of the _____ field and find an empty bench _____ near the woods. I like to blend into the _____ of the park and watch other people.

Today, I saw a college student sitting under a tree and reading a _____. There were a few old ladies on another bench looking at a _____ filled with photographs of themselves from their childhood. A _____ of mine from school whizzed past them on a _____.

The bleachers of the _____ were deserted. The sunlit park was quiet except for the sudden roar of a _____ speeding down the _____ near the park. I decided to take out a pen and a _____ from my backpack. This seemed like a good time to _____ ideas for a story I have to write.

Lesson 31 Compound Words

Fun with Words

Write the spelling word that completes each sign and includes one word from the underlined compound word.

1. Please don't <u>jaywalk</u>! Use the _____ instead.

2. We need to paint the <u>outline</u> of the field to make each end

_____.

3. Buy tickets to the fair at the <u>newsstand</u> next to the _____.

4. Come and enjoy the scenic _____ of our <u>campground</u>.

5. Shop here for a new bicycle, <u>surfboard</u>, or _____!

6. Buy one ticket and your <u>teammate</u> or _____ gets one.

7. Make sure you bring your <u>textbook</u> and a _____ to class.

8. The <u>football</u> field and the _____ court are closed.

Words Across the Curriculum

Say each science word. Then, write the word.

1. earthquake _____   **3.** waterfall _____

2. rattlesnake _____   **4.** heartbeat _____

Write the missing science words.

1. A _____ make a warning sound with its tail.

2. During exercise, a person's _____ becomes faster.

3. A severe _____ can destroy buildings, roads, and bridges.

4. A _____ forms when a stream rushes over rocks that resist erosion.

Lesson 31 Compound Words

Words in Writing

Write a description of a hobby that you enjoy. Use at least four words from the box.

_____

_____

_____

_____

_____

highway	motorcycle	stoplight	grandstand	waterfall
football	newspaper	sideline	brainstorm	rattlesnake
classmate	background	crosswalk	scrapbook	heartbeat
skateboard	notebook	somewhere	earthquake	

Misspelled Words

Read the description. Circle the five misspelled words. Then, write the words correctly.

I like to collect photos and newpaper clippings for my scrapebook. I include articles about my brother's football team. I have a photo of my dad riding his motercycle on the hiway. I also have a photo of myself on the skatboard I got for my birthday.

_____ _____ _____

_____ _____

Review Lessons 27–31

Write the spelling word that names each number.

1. 19   _____

2. 40   _____

3. 11   _____

4. 13   _____

5. 20   _____

6. 15   _____

7. 1,000,000   _____

8. 30   _____

Write the spelling word that is an antonym of each word or phrase.

9. most beautiful   _____

10. combined   _____

11. lighter   _____

12. pain   _____

13. sad   _____

14. dryness   _____

15. answer   _____

16. no place   _____

17. sunniest   _____

18. most sorrowful   _____

Review Lessons 27–31

Write the spelling word that fits with each group of words.

19. hockey, soccer, _____

20. million, trillion, _____

21. rugs, curtains, _____

22. republic, country, _____

23. shape, outline, _____

24. bicycle, scooter, _____

25. year, decade, _____

26. street, road, _____

27. safety, preservation, _____

28. trait, characteristic, _____

Write the spelling word that is a synonym of each word.

29. ideas _____

30. setting _____

31. beast _____

32. dozen _____

33. stadium _____

34. place _____

A

ac·tors *pl. n.* People who act in plays, movies, television shows, and other media, usually in fictional roles.

ad·dress *n.* The location to which mail or goods can be sent to a person. *v.* To speak to.

ad·ven·ture *n.* An exciting, dangerous, or unusual experience.

af·ford *v.* To have enough money to spare; to be able to provide.

a·gainst *prep.* In contact with; not in favor of or in combat with.

a·gent *n.* A person who acts as the representative of another.

a·lign *v.* To adjust or bring into line.

al·though *conj.* Even though; despite the fact that.

a·maze *v.* To overwhelm with surprise or wonder.

an·gle *n.* A shape made by two straight lines meeting at a point.

an·kle *n.* The joint that connects the foot with the leg.

an·swer *n.* A written or spoken reply, as to a question; a result or solution, as to a problem. *v.* To respond.

art·ists' *pl. poss.* Belonging to people who practice the fine arts of painting, sculpture, architecture, literature, music, dance, or theater.

at·tack *v.* To apply force or to assault; to work on energetically. *n.* A sudden action of aggression; assault.

at·ten·tion *n.* Observation, notice, or mental concentration.

a·while *adv.* For a short time.

B

ba·bies' *poss. pl.* Belonging to infants or very young children.

back·ground *n.* The area or surface behind which objects are represented.

ba·con *n.* Meat from the side and back of a pig.

badge *n.* A symbol worn for identification.

bal·ance *n.* The state of a body or object having a steady position; a tool for determining the weight of something. *v.* To keep in a steady state or position.

ban·ner *n.* A piece of cloth with a symbol or message on it, such as a flag.

bare·ly *adv.* Scarcely; hardly.

bas·ket *n.* A container made of woven material.

beast *n.* Any animal other than a human, especially a large, four-legged animal.

beau·ti·ful *adj.* Being pleasing to the eye.

beet *n.* The root from a cultivated plant that can be used as a vegetable.

be·fore *adv.* Earlier; previously. *prep.* In front of.

be·have *v.* To act or function in a certain manner.

be·lieve *v.* To accept as true or real.

be·low *adv.* In or to a lower place. *prep.* Lower in rank, degree, or position.

bi·cy·cle *n.* A two-wheeled vehicle propelled by pedals.

bil·lion *n.* A thousand million.

bi·og·ra·phy *n.* A researched and accurate report of the life and accomplishments of a person written by another person.

bi·ome *n.* A major type of habitat, such as a jungle or grasslands.

blan·ket *n.* A covering used on a bed for warmth; something that evenly covers a surface.

bor·der *n.* A political or geographic boundary; a decorative or protective margin or edge.

bot·tom *n.* The lowest or deepest part of anything.

brain *n.* The main organ of the body's nervous system, responsible for control of the body, the senses, and coordination; the center of thought and emotion.

brain·storm *n.* A sudden idea or inspiration. *v.* To think and contribute ideas without boundaries.

brave *adj.* Having courage; willing to face danger or pain.

breathe *v.* To draw air into and expel from the lungs.

breath·less *adj.* Without breath.

bridge *n.* A structure allowing passage over two bodies of land divided by water or some other gap.

broke *v.* Past tense of *break.* Cracked or split into pieces; caused to end.

broth·ers' *pl. poss.* Belonging to males who share the same parents as another person.

bub·ble *n.* A small body of gas contained inside a liquid.

buck·et *n.* A vessel used to carry liquids or solids; a pail.

built *v.* Past tense of build. Created or fashioned.

bunch *n.* A cluster or group of like items.

C

cab·bage *n.* A vegetable similar in shape to lettuce.

ca·bin *n.* A shelter in the woods, usually made of logs.

ca·ble *adj.* Sent through wires or a satellite. *n.* A heavy rope made from fiber or steel.

cac·tus *n.* A plant that lives primarily in desert regions.

cal·ves *pl. n.* Young offspring of cows.

cam·er·a *n.* A device for taking photographs.

can·dle *n.* A wax form with a wick used for light.

ca·pac·i·ty *n.* The maximum amount of matter, especially liquid, that a container can hold.

car·bon *n.* A nonmetallic element that is present in all living and once-living material.

care·less *adj.* Without care or concern.

car·pet *n.* A thick, woven floor covering.

cau·tion *n.* Care regarding danger or risk; a warning advising careful planning or procedure.

ceil·ing *n.* The overhead covering of a room.

cel·e·brate *v.* To observe with ceremonies, rejoicing, or festivity.

cel·er·y *n.* A green vegetable with an edible stalk.

cen·tral *adj.* In, near, or at the center.

ce·re·al *n.* An edible grain eaten as a breakfast food.

cer·tain *adj.* Very sure; without any doubt.

cer·tain·ly *adv.* Definitely.

chance *n.* The possibility of something happening; opportunity.

chap·ter *n.* A major division of a book.

charge *v.* To ask a price for something. *n.* The required price; the amount of electrical energy that an object has.

cheap *adj.* Inexpensive; low in cost; of poor quality.

cheer·ful *adj.* Having or being in good spirits.

cheese *n.* A food made from milk.

cher·ry *n.* A small, round, deep red or purplish red fruit with a small, hard stone.

chief *n.* The person of highest rank *adj.* Most important.

child·ren's *pl. poss.* Belonging to young people.

choke *v.* To prevent or interrupt the breathing.

chore *n.* A daily task.

cir·cus *n.* A traveling show featuring clowns, acrobats, trained animals, and other acts.

cit·i·zen *n.* A resident of a town, city, or country.

class·mate *n.* A member of one's class.

cli·mate *n.* The weather conditions of a certain region.

close *v.* To shut.

close·ly *adv.* Being near in time, space, or relationship.

clos·et *n.* A small cabinet, compartment, or room for storage.

clothes *n.* Articles made from cloth and worn on the body.

cloud·i·er *adj.* having more clouds than another.

cloud·i·est *adj.* Having the most clouds of all.

cloud·y *adj.* Having clouds.

color·ful *adj.* Having many colors.

col·umn *n.* A vertical list of numbers; a pillar used in constructing buildings.

comb *n.* A toothed device used for smoothing and arranging hair.

com·pound *n.* A mixture made of two or more parts or substances.

con·di·tion *n.* The state of existence of a person or object.

con·tin·ue *v.* To maintain without interruption a course or condition.

cor·ner *n.* The point formed when two surfaces or lines meet and form an angle.

cot·ton *n.* A plant grown for its soft, fluffy fibers, which are used to make cloth; the fabric made from the fibers of such a plant.

course *n.* The act of moving in a path from one point to another.

court *n.* A place where justice is carried out and trials are held; an area marked off for playing a sport.

crea·ture *n.* Any living being, especially a member of the animal kingdom.

crick·et *n.* A leaping insect.

croak *n.* A hoarse, raspy cry such as that made by a frog.

cross·walk *n.* A marked area of a street, usually at an intersection, for people to cross.

cur·rent *n.* a stream within a body of water or air that constantly flows in the same path. *adj.* Belonging or occurring in the present time.

curve *n.* A line that has a smooth slope.

cus·tom *n.* An accepted practice of a community or people.

cus·to·mers' *poss. pl.* Belonging to people who buy items from sellers.

cy·cle *n.* A series of events that occur repeatedly.

cyl·in·der *n.* A long, round object that is either hollow or solid.

D

dai·ly *adj.* Happening every day.

danc·ers' *poss. pl.* Belonging to people who move their bodies to music.

dan·ger *n.* Something unsafe, causing injury or loss.

dan·ger·ous *adj.* Having danger.

de·cide *v.* To settle; to make up one's mind.

dec·i·mal *n.* A proper fraction based on the number

10 and indicated by the use of a decimal point.

de·gree *n.* A unit of cold or heat on a thermometer.

des·ert *n.* A hot, dry, barren region of land that receives very little rainfall.

de·sign *n.* A plan or sketch made to serve as a guide; a pattern. *v.* To invent or create in the mind; to draw and sketch an idea or outline.

dif·fer·ent *adj.* Not the same.

di·no·saur *n.* Any extinct reptile from prehistoric times.

di·rec·tion *n.* An instruction, order or command; the path or line along which something points.

dis·a·gree *v.* To vary in opinion; to differ; to argue.

dis·ap·pear *v.* To vanish; to drop from sight.

dis·ap·point *v.* To fail to satisfy; to let down.

dis·cov·er *v.* To make known or visible; to find for the first time.

dis·cuss *v.* To hold a conversation; to talk.

dis·ease *n.* A sickness, often spread from one person to another.

dis·hon·est *adj.* Lacking honesty; coming from falseness.

dis·like *v.* To have no appreciation or respect for something.

dis·miss *v.* To allow to leave; to remove from a position.

dis·play *n.* An exhibit. *v.* To show or put on exhibit.

dis·tance *n.* Separation in time or space.

dis·trib·ute *v.* To divide among many.

dis·turb *v.* To destroy the balance or rest of someone or something.

ditch *n.* A trench in the ground.

di·vide *v.* To separate into halves or portions and give out in shares.

dou·ble *adj.* Twice as much.

drive *v.* To operate a vehicle.

du·ty *n.* Something a person must or ought to do; an obligation or responsibility.

E

ea·ger·ly *adv.* With desire.

ear·ly *adj.* Occurring near the beginning of a period of time; before the expected time.

Earth *n.* The third planet from the sun.

earth·quake *n.* A sudden movement of Earth's crust that causes violent shaking on the surface of Earth.

ef·fort *n.* An attempt; a use of physical or mental energy to do something.

eigh·teen *n.* The number after seventeen and before nineteen.

eighth *n.* Number eight in a series.

e·lec·tric *adj.* Relating to energy, especially energy carried by protons and electrons through wires.

el·e·ment *n.* A substance that contains only one type of atoms.

e·lev·en *n.* The number after ten and before twelve.

en·er·gy *n.* The ability or power to move or work.

English *n.* A language spoken and written in the United States, England, and other parts of the world.

e·nough *adj.* Adequate to satisfy demands or needs.

e·qua·tor *n.* The imaginary circle around Earth that separates the northern and southern hemispheres.

es·cape *v.* To break free from capture or restraint.

es·pe·cial·ly *adv.* Gaining or deserving special consideration.

e·vent·ful *adv.* Full of happenings.

eve·ry·one *pron.* All persons.

ex·act·ly *adv.* Accurately or precisely; perfectly.

ex·am·ine *v.* To observe or inspect.

ex·am·ple *n.* A representative as a sample.

ex·cel·lent *adj.* Of the best quality.

ex·cept *prep.* But; with the omission or exclusion of.

ex·cit·ing *adj.* Fun-filled; entertaining.

ex·cuse *n.* A reason given to explain something.

ex·er·cise *n.* A physical workout; a drill or repeated activity to gain skill.

ex·ert *v.* To make a strenuous effort.

ex·haust·ed *adj.* Extremely tired.

ex·hib·it *n.* A display. *v.* To display, or put up for public view.

ex·it *n.* A way or passage out.

ex·pect *v.* To look forward to something as probable or certain.

ex·pen·sive *adj.* Costing a lot of money; high-priced.

ex·per·i·ment *n.* An act or test performed to demonstrate or illustrate a truth.

ex·pert *n.* A person having great knowledge, experience, or skill in a certain field.

ex·plain *v.* To make understandable; to make clear.

ex·plode *v.* To burst or blow up violently with a loud noise.

ex·plore *v.* To examine and investigate in a systematic way.

ex·port *v.* To carry or send goods or raw materials to other countries for resale or trade.

ex·press *v.* To put into words; to show outwardly through words, actions, or art.

ex·tend *v.* To stretch or open to full length.

ex·tra *adj.* Over and above what is normal, required, or expected.

ex·treme·ly *adv.* To a great or excessive degree.

F

faith·ful *adj.* True and trustworthy in the performance of duty, promises, or obligations.

fam·i·lies' *poss. pl.* belonging to groups of parents and their children.

fea·ture *n.* An important part or characteristic of something; a part of the face.

fetch *v.* To go after and return with.

field *n.* A piece of land with few or no trees; an area of land cleared and set aside for the playing of a sport.

fif·teen *n.* The number after fourteen and before sixteen.

fif·ty *n.* The number after forty-nine and before fifty-one.

fight *n.* A struggle or argument. *v.* To struggle against in combat; to quarrel; to argue.

fig·ure *n.* The visible form of something; the human form or body.

fin·al·ly *adv.* At last; after a long time.

fin·ish *v.* To bring to or reach an end.

fla·vor *n.* A distinctive taste of something.

flute *n.* A high-pitched musical woodwind instrument.

foot·ball *n.* A team game whose object is to get the ball over a goal line or between goalposts by running, passing or kicking; the ball used in such a game.

force *n.* Energy or power; strength; *v.* To compel or make happen by force.

for·ty *n.* The number after thirty-nine and after forty-one.

fort *n.* A building used as protection against an army.

four·teen *n.* The number after thirteen and before fifteen.

fowl *n.* A bird used as food or hunted as game.

frac·tion *n.* A small part; in mathematics, an indicated quantity less than a whole number.

free·ly *adv.* Without being held back or restrained; with an easy manner.

friends' *poss. pl.* Belonging to people personally well-known and liked.

fright·ful *adj.* Causing fear; disgusting or shocking.

fur·ni·ture *n.* Movable articles, such as chairs and tables, used in a home, office, or other interior.

fur·ther *adj.* Beyond; more distant in time or space.

G

gar·bage *n.* Trash or waste material.

gath·er *v.* To bring or come together into one place or group.

gen·tle *adj.* Not harsh, severe, rough, or loud.

geese *pl. n.* More than one goose.

germ *n.* A tiny living organism, especially one that causes disease.

gov·ern·ment *n.* An organization that rules or directs a country, state, or city.

grace·ful *adj.* Full of seemingly effortless beauty and charm of movement.

grand·moth·ers' *pl. poss. n.* Belonging to the mothers of people's fathers or mothers.

grand·stand *n.* A seating area for people to view an outdoor event.

graph *n.* A diagram that represents the relationship between sets of things.

great *adj.* Very large in size or volume.

groan *n.* A long, deep sound of pain or disapproval. *v.* To utter a deep, prolonged sound of pain or disapproval.

grown *adj.* Having matured or increased in size.

guess *n.* An opinion formed without complete knowledge. *v.* To make a judgment or form an opinion on uncertain or incomplete knowledge.

gyp·sy *n.* A member of a nomadic group of people.

H

halves *n.* Two equal parts of a whole.

ham·ster's *poss. n.* Belonging to a large rodent with large cheek pouches and a short tail.

hap·pen *v.* To occur or come to pass.

hap·pi·er *adj.* More happy than another.

hap·pi·est *adj.* Most happy of all.

hap·py *adj.* Enjoying contentment and well-being.

harm·less *adj.* Unable to cause pain.

health·i·er *adj.* In a better state or having better health than another.

health·i·est *adj.* In the best state or having the best health of all.

healthy *adj.* Being in good physical condition.

heart·beat *n.* A pulsation of the heart.

heav·i·er *adj.* Weighing more than another.

heav·i·est *adj.* Weighing more than all others.

heav·y *adj.* Of great weight.

heel *n.* The rounded back part of the human foot under and behind the ankle.

height *n.* The distance from the bottom to the top of something.

high·way *n.* A main road connecting towns and cities.

his·to·ry *n.* Past events, especially those involving human affairs.

hitch *v.* To fasten or tie temporarily with a knot.

hock·ey *n.* A game played on ice between two teams of skaters.

hol·low *adj.* Having a cavity or empty space inside.

hon·ey *n.* A sweet, sticky substance made by bees from the nectar gathered from flowers.

hope·ful *adj.* Having belief that something can happen.

hunch *v.* To bend or stoop.

hur·ry *v.* To move or cause to move with haste.

hy·dro·gen *n.* A colorless, normally odorless, highly flammable gas.

I

i·ci·cle *n.* A hanging spike of ice formed by dripping water that freezes.

im·age *n.* A representation of the form and features of someone or something.

in·clude *v.* To have as a part or member.

in·com·plete *adj.* Not finished.

in·cor·rect *adj.* Wrong; not correct.

in·spect *v.* To examine or look at very carefully for flaws.

in·stant *n.* A very short time; a moment.

in·stead *adv.* Rather than something else.

in·stinct *n.* A tendency for an animal to act in a certain way that is inherited, not learned.

in·ter·sect *v.* To divide by cutting through or across.

in·vent *v.* To create by an original effort or design.

in·vite *v.* To request the presence or participation of a person.

is·land *n.* A piece of land smaller than a continent and completely surrounded by water.

is·sue *n.* A subject that is under discussion or consideration.

J

jazz *n.* A kind of music that has a strong rhythmic structure.

jew·el *n.* A precious stone.

jock·ey *n.* A person who rides a horse in races as a profession.

jum·ble *n.* A confused or disordered mixture. *v.* To mix in a confused mass.

junk *n.* Discarded or unused items.

ju·ry *n.* A group of people summoned to serve at a court trial to give a verdict according to evidence presented.

jus·tice *n.* The principle of moral or ideal rightness.

K

kan·ga·roo *n.* A jumping marsupial of Australia, with short forelegs, large hind limbs, and a large tail.

ket·tle *n.* A large, metal pot for stewing or boiling.

kni·ves *pl. n.* Tools used to cut items.

L

land·form *n.* A feature of land, such as a mountain or cliff.

la·sa·gna *n.* Pasta in the shape of long strips.

least *adj.* The smallest amount.

leaves *pl. n.* More than one leaf.

lem·on *n.* An oval, yellow citrus fruit grown on a tree.

li·brar·y *n.* A collection of books, pamphlets, magazines, and reference books kept for reading.

light·ning *n.* The flash of light produced by a high-tension natural electric discharge into the atmosphere.

limb *n.* A large branch of a tree; an animal's appendage used for movement or grasping; an arm or leg.

lives *pl. n.* More than one life.

loaves *pl. n.* More than one loaf, such as a loaf of bread.

lo·cal *adj.* Pertaining to, being in, or serving a particular area or place.

lo·ca·tion *n.* A particular place.

lodge *n.* A house, such as a cabin, used as a temporary or seasonal dwelling.

lone·ly *adj.* Being without companions.

lug·gage *n.* Suitcases or other baggage used to carry items when traveling.

M

ma·chine *n.* A device or system built to use energy to do work.

man·age *v.* To direct or control the affairs or use of a place or event.

mean *v.* To have in mind as a purpose or intent. *adj.* Not nice. *n.* The average of a set of numbers.

meas·ure *v.* To determine the range, dimension, size, or capacity of anything.

me·di·an *n.* The middle number in a set of numbers arranged from least to greatest.

men·tion *v.* To refer to in passing or briefly.

mes·sage *n.* Any information, command, or news transmitted from one person to another.

met·al *n.* One of a category of hard solids, such as steel.

mice *pl. n.* Small rodents.

mild *adj.* Gentle in manner, behavior, or disposition; not severe or extreme.

mil·lion *n.* A number equal to 1,000 x 1,000.

min·er *n.* One who works underground in search of material, such as coal.

mi·nor *adj.* Not of legal age; lesser in degree, size, or importance.

mis·er·y *n.* A state of great unhappiness, distress, or pain.

mis·for·tune *n.* Bad luck or fortune.

mis·plac·ed *v.* Mislaid; put in a wrong place.

mis·print *n.* An error in a publication, such as a newspaper or book.

mis·quote *v.* To repeat incorrectly what someone has said.

mis·spell·ed *adj.* Not spelled right. *v.* Spelled a word wrongly.

mis·take *n.* An error; a wrong statement, action, or decision.

mod·el *n.* A small representation of an object.

mois·ture *n.* The presence of a small amount of liquid; dampness.

mo·ment *n.* A few seconds; a very short amount of time.

mon·key *n.* A member of the primates, excluding humans, having a long tail.

month·ly *adj.* Occurring, done, or payable each month.

mo·tion *n.* The act or process of changing position.

mo·tion·less *adj.* Not moving.

mo·tor *n.* A device that powers a machine.

mo·tor·cy·cle *n.* A two-wheeled vehicle powered by a motor.

moun·tain *n.* A land mass that rises above its surroundings and is higher than a hill.

mul·ti·ple *adj.* A number that is a product of a certain number and another number.

mus·cle *n.* Body tissue made of long cells that contract and produce movement.

mu·sic *n.* Pleasing or harmonious combinations of sounds.

N

nap·kin *n.* A cloth or soft paper, used while eating, for wiping the lips and fingers.

na·tion *n.* A group of people who are represented by one government.

nat·u·ral *adj.* Produced or existing by nature.

neigh·bor *n.* One who lives near another.

news·pa·per *n.* A weekly or daily publication that contains recent information.

nine·teen *n.* The number after eighteen and before twenty.

no·ble *adj.* Morally good.

nor·mal *adj.* Ordinary, average, usual.

note·book *n.* Sheets of paper bound together and used for writing.

no·tice *v.* To be aware of; to observe or pay attention to.

nu·mer·al *n.* A symbol or figure, or a group of these that represents a number.

O

o·cean *n.* A huge body of salt water.

of·fice *n.* A place where people perform business or professional duties.

or·der *n.* A command. *v.* To command; to demand.

or·gan *n.* A part of an animal, human, or plant that performs a specific function.

o·ver *prep.* Above; across; upon.

oxen *pl. n.* Plural form of *ox.*

P

pack·age *n.* One or more items packed, wrapped, or bound together.

paint·ers' *poss. pl.* Belonging to people who paint.

palm *n.* The inner area of the hand between the fingers and the wrist.

pan·ic *n.* A sudden, uncontrollable fear. *v.* To be overcome by a sudden, uncontrollable fear.

pa·per *n.* A substance made of pulp from wood, used for writing upon.

par·ti·cle *n.* A very small piece of solid matter.

patch *n.* A piece of fabric used to repair a weakened or torn area in a garment.

peak *n.* The summit of a mountain; the top.

pearl *n.* A round, whitish gem formed inside an oyster.

peek *v.* To look at shyly or quickly, often from a place of hiding.

perch *n.* A place on which birds rest; any place for standing or sitting. *v.* To rest or sit upon.

per·fect *adj.* Having no defect or fault.

per·fect·ly *adv.* Having no defect or fault.

per·son *n.* A human being.

per·son·al·ly *adv.* In person; face to face.

pic·nic *n.* An outdoor social gathering with food.

pinch *v.* To squeeze between a finger and thumb, causing pain or discomfort.

plain *adj.* Ordinary; not rich or luxurious; not beautiful or highly decorated.

plas·tic *n.* A human-made material molded and then hardened into objects.

pleas·ure *n.* A feeling of satisfaction or enjoyment.

plunge *v.* To thrust or cast something, as into water.

pol·ish *v.* To make shiny and smooth by rubbing.

poor *adj.* Lacking possessions and money.

pore *n.* A tiny opening, as in the skin.

port *n.* A city or town with a harbor for loading and unloading cargo from ships.

por·trait *n.* A painting of a person.

pos·si·ble *adj.* Capable of being true, happening, or being accomplished.

pour *v.* To drop a liquid into another container.

pred·a·tor *n.* An animal that survives by eating other animals.

pret·ti·er *adj.* More attractive than others.

pret·ti·est *adj.* Most attractive of all.

pret·ty *adj.* Pleasant; attractive.

price *n.* The set amount of money expected or given for the sale of something; cost.

prism *n.* A solid figure with triangular ends and rectangular sides, used to disperse light into a spectrum.

pri·vate *adj.* Secluded or removed from the public view.

prob·a·bly *adv.* Most likely.

prod·uct *n.* Something produced, manufactured, or obtained.

prom·ise *n.* An assurance given that one will or will not do something; a pledge. *v.* To declare that one will or will not do something.

proof *n.* Evidence that supports a fact or shows that something is true.

pro·pose *v.* To present or put forward for consideration or action.

pro·tec·tion *n.* Something that shields a person, animal, or thing from harm; the act of keeping safe from harm.

pro·ton *n.* An atomic particle with a positive charge.

pub·lish *v.* To print and distribute books, magazines, or newspapers to the public.

punch *n.* A drink made from different substances, often fruit juice. *v.* To hit sharply with the hand or fist.

pur·pose *n.* A desired goal; an intention.

puz·zle *n.* A mystery or riddle. *v.* To bewilder; to confuse.

Q

ques·tion *n.* An expression of inquiry that requires an answer. *v.* To ask.

quite *adv.* To the fullest degree; really; actually; to a great extent.

R

rack·et *n.* An instrument used to play tennis.

ra·di·us *n.* A line from the center of a circle to its surface.

ranch *n.* A large establishment for raising cattle, sheep, or other livestock.

range *n.* The limits between which something varies or changes; a tract of land over which animals such as cattle and horses graze.

rap·id·ly *adv.* With great speed.

rat·tle·snake *n.* A poisonous reptile with segments at the end of its tail that make a rattling sound.

re·act *v.* To act in response to.

reason *n.* The explanation for doing something.

re·cent·ly *adv.* In the near past; not long ago.

rec·og·nize *v.* To experience or identify something or someone as having been known previously.

re·cord *v.* To write down for future use or permanent reference.

re·cy·cle *v.* To make suitable for reuse.

re·fuse *v.* To decline or reject; to strongly state unwillingness to do something.

re·gret *v.* To feel disappointed or sorry about.

reg·u·lar *adj.* Usual; normal; conforming to a set of principles or procedures.

re·mem·ber *v.* To bring back or recall to the mind.

re·move *v.* To take off or away; to get rid of.

re·peat *v.* To do again.

re·port *n.* A detailed account about observations. *v.* To give a detailed account or statement.

re·spect·ful *adv.* Full of consideration or courtesy for.

rest·less *adv.* Nervous; unable to rest.

re·treat *n.* A place where one can rest and relax; the act of withdrawing from danger. *v.* To withdraw, as from battle.

re·turn *v.* To come back to an earlier place or condition.

re·view *v.* To study or look over something again.

ri·ver *n.* A large stream.

ro·tate *v.* To turn on an axis.

roy·al *adj.* Relating to a king or queen.

S

safe·ly *adv.* In a way without danger.

sal·ad *n.* A dish usually made of green vegetables,

fruit, or meat tossed with dressing.

sand·wich *n.* Two or more slices of bread with a filling, such as cheese or meat, placed between them.

scale *n.* A device for weighing; a flat plate that covers certain animals, especially fish and reptiles.

scarves *pl. n.* Wide pieces of cloth used to keep the neck warm.

scent *n.* A smell; an odor.

sci·ence *n.* The study and explanation of things and events in nature and in the universe.

scram·ble *v.* To move with panic.

scrap·book *n.* A book for collecting photos, various paper items, or other flat objects.

scrape *n.* a mark left on a surface by the rubbing of something against it; a minor cut on the skin. *v.* To rub or move roughly along a surface.

scream *n.* A sharp cry of fear or pain. *v.* To utter a long, sharp cry, as of fear or pain.

screech *v.* To make a shrill, harsh noise.

screw *n.* A metal piece that resembles a nail, having a spiral thread used for fastening things together.

scrib·ble *v.* To write without thought or care to penmanship.

search *v.* To try to find something.

se·cret·ly *adv.* In a hidden or mysterious manner.

select *v.* To choose or pick out.

sen·tence *n.* A series of words arranged to express a complete thought.

sep·a·rate *adj.* Apart from others.

set·tle *v.* To colonize; to adjust or place in a proper position; to make quiet or calm.

se·ven·teen *n.* The number after sixteen and before eighteen.

sheep *n.* A herding mammal with thick, wooly fur.

shel·ter *n.* Something that gives protection or cover.

shel·ves *pl. n.* Surfaces for storing objects, such as books or dishes.

shield *n.* A piece of protective metal or wood held in front of the body. *v.* To protect.

shift *n.* A period of working. *v.* To change direction or position.

shirt *n.* A garment worn on the upper part of the body.

side·line *n.* The edge of a court or sports field that marks its limits.

sight *n.* The ability to see with the eyes; an image seen with the eyes.

signal *n.* An action or symbol that warns, directs, or informs. *v.* To make a sign of warning or instruction.

si·lent *adj.* Making no sound.

sim·ple *adj.* Easy to do or understand.

site *n.* A location, as of a city, building, or historical event.

six·teen *n.* The number after fifteen and before seventeen.

skate·board *n.* A narrow piece of wood with wheels attached for a person to move along a concrete surface.

sketch *n.* A rough drawing or outline. *v.* To make a rough drawing or outline.

slight *adj.* Minor; unimportant.

smooth *adj.* Having an even surface; flat; without irregularity.

snatch *v.* To seize or grasp something suddenly.

sock·et *n.* A hollow opening into which something is fitted; an electrical outlet.

sol·id *adj.* Having a definite, firm shape and volume. *n.* A three-dimensional figure.

sol·u·tion *n.* An answer to a problem; a combination of liquids.

some·where *n.* An unspecified place.

sor·ry *adj.* Feeling or showing sympathy or regret.

source *n.* Any point of origin or beginning.

spark·le *v.* To give off light.

special *adj.* Unusual, exceptional, or uncommon.

spe·cies *n.* A group of animals or plants that share the same characteristics and can mate with other members of the same species.

spoke *n.* One of the rods that serve to connect and support the rim of a wheel. *v.* Past tense of *speak*; talked.

spot·less *adj.* Perfectly clean; without flaws.

squash *n.* An edible fruit of the gourd family. *v.* To press or squeeze into a soft pulp.

squeak·y *adj.* Having a sharp, penetrating sound.

squid *n.* A type of ten-armed marine animal with a tapered body.

squirm *v.* To twist the body in a wiggling motion.

stat·ue *n.* A form sculpted from wood, clay, metal, or stone.

steak *n.* A piece of meat, usually from a cow, cooked and eaten.

steam *n.* Water in the form of vapor, caused by heat.

stew *n.* A mixture of food, usually meat and vegetables, cooked on low heat for a long period of time. *v.* To cook slowly; to simmer; to boil.

stom·ach *n.* The organ of the body into which food passes from the esophagus to begin the process of digestion; belly, abdomen.

stop·light *n.* A signalling device that controls the flow of automobile traffic at intersections.

strap *n.* A long, narrow strip of leather or other material used to secure objects.

straw *n.* A stalk of dried, threshed grain; a slender, plastic or paper tube used to suck up a liquid.

streak *n.* A line or mark that is a different color from the surrounding area.

strength *n.* The quality of being strong.

stretch *v.* To extend fully.

string *n.* A strip of thin twine or wire.

sud·den *adj.* Happening very quickly without warning or notice.

sug·gest *v.* To give an idea for action or consideration.

suit *n.* A set of clothes to be worn together.

sun·nier *adj.* Having more sunlight than other places.

sun·niest *adj.* Having the most sunlight of all places.

sup·ply *v.* To provide with what is needed; to make available.

sup·port *v.* To bear or hold the weight of.

sure *adj.* Certain; being impossible to doubt.

sur·face *n.* The exterior or outside boundary of something.

surge *v.* To increase suddenly. *n.* A burst, as of water or energy.

surprise *v.* To startle.

swal·low *v.* To cause food to pass from the mouth to the stomach.

sweet *adj.* Having a sugary, agreeable flavor.

sym·bol *n.* Something that stands for or represents something else.

ta·ble *n.* An article of furniture having a flat top, supported by legs.

tem·per·a·ture *n.* A measure of heat or cold in

relation to the body or environment.

ter·ri·ble *adj.* Horrible; causing fear or terror.

thank·ful *adj.* Grateful; feeling or showing gratitude.

them·selves *pron.* Them or they.

thieves *pl. n.* People who steal; robbers.

thirst·y *adj.* Having a need or desire for a drink of water or other refreshing liquid.

thir·teen *n.* The number after twelve and before fourteen.

thirty *n.* The number after twenty-nine and before thirty-one.

thought·ful *adj.* Showing care or consideration for another; engaged in thinking.

threat *n.* An expression or warning of harm.

thrill *n.* A feeling of sudden, intense excitement, fear, or joy.

throat *n.* The front section or part of the neck containing passages for food and air.

throne *n.* The chair on which a ruler sits.

through *prep.* From the beginning to the end; in one side and out the other; by means of.

throw *v.* To toss or fling through the air.

tick·et *n.* A printed slip of paper or cardboard allowing its holder to enter a specified event or to enjoy a privilege.

tide *n.* The rise and fall of the surface level of the ocean.

ti·tle *n.* An identifying name of a book, poem, play, or other creative work; a word used with a person's name to show respect, a profession, or rank.

tomb *n.* A vault for burying the dead; a grave.

to·tal·ly *adv.* Completely.

touch *n.* The sense by which objects are observed by contact with the skin. *v.* To allow a part of the body, as the hands, to feel something else; to come in contact with.

tow·el *n.* An absorbent piece of cloth used for drying or wiping.

traf·fic *n.* The passage or movement of vehicles.

trav·el *v.* To journey or move from one place to another.

treat *n.* A pleasant surprise. *v.* To behave or act toward.

trem·ble *v.* To shake, as with fear or from cold.

trick·le *n.* A small stream, as of water. *v.* To flow in droplets or a small stream.

troop *n.* A group or assembly of people.

trop·ic·al *adj.* Being hot and humid in climate.

trou·ble *n.* Difficulty or danger; something that causes a problem.

truce *n.* A temporary end to fighting or a disagreement.

tru·ly *adj.* Really, actually; certainly.

twelve *n.* The number after eleven and before thirteen.

twenty *n.* The number after nineteen and before twenty-one.

twitch *v.* To move or cause to move in a jerky manner.

U

ug·li·er *adj.* More unpleasant to look at than others.

ug·li·est *adj.* Most unpleasant to look at than all others.

ug·ly *adj.* Offensive or unpleasant to look at.

um·brel·la *n.* A collapsible frame covered with plastic or cloth, held above the head as protection from sun or rain.

un·a·ble *adj.* Not having the necessary capabilities, skills, or power.

un·a·ware *adj.* Not realizing.

un·earth *v.* To discover; to dig up.

un·fair *adj.* Not just; not following accepted rules.

u·ni·form *n.* Identical clothing worn by the members of a group.

u·ni·ty *n.* The fact or state of being one.

un·less *conj.* Only with the condition that something else happens.

un·til *prep.* Up to the time of.

up·per *adj.* Higher in status, position, or location.

u·su·al·ly *adv.* Happening regularly or often.

V

va·ca·tion *n.* A period of time away from work for pleasure, relaxation, or rest.

val·ley *n.* Low land between ranges of hills or mountains.

val·ue *n.* The worth or cost of something. *v.* To appreciate or consider as being important.

vic·tim *n.* A person who is harmed or killed; a person who is tricked or cheated by another person.

vi·ta·min *n.* Any of various substances found in foods that are essential to good health.

vol·can·o *n.* A mountain through which lava is forced out.

W

waist *n.* The narrow part of the body between the chest and hips.

waste *n.* Worthless material or trash; the act of carelessly using up something. *v.* To use up carelessly.

wa·ter *n.* The clear liquid making up oceans, lakes, and streams.

wa·ter·fall *n.* A flowing body of water, such as a river or stream, falling from a height.

weath·er *n.* The condition of the air or atmosphere in terms of humidity, temperature, and similar features.

week·ly *adv.* Once a week.

weight *n.* The amount of heaviness of something.

whose *pron.* Belonging to or having to do with one's belongings.

win·dow *n.* An opening built into a wall for light and air; a pane of glass.

wise·ly *adv.* In an intelligent manner.

wives *pl. n.* Married women.

wolves *pl. n.* More than one wolf.

won·der·ful *adj.* Very good or excellent; causing amazement.

wor·ry *v.* To be concerned or troubled.

worth·less *adj.* Having no worth or value.

wreath *n.* A decorative, ringlike form of intertwined flowers, bows, and other articles.

wreck *v.* To crash into something; to ruin.

wren *n.* A small, brown songbird.

wrench *n.* A tool used to secure bolts.

wrin·kle *n.* A small crease on the skin or on fabric.

Y

young *adj.* Of or relating to the early stage of life; not old.

Parts of Speech

adj. = adjective
adv. = adverb
art. = article
conj. = conjunction
n. = noun
prep. = preposition
pron. = pronoun
v. = verb

Page 6

Say each word. Listen for the short **a** sound and the short **e** sound. Then, write the word.

Spelling Tip	The short **a** and short **e** sounds often come between two consonants. The symbol for the short **a** sound is /a/. The symbol for the short **e** sound is /e/.

Spelling Words

sandwich	sandwich
blanket	blanket
effort	effort
package	package
extra	extra
traffic	traffic
napkin	napkin
panic	panic
basket	basket
address	address
cabin	cabin
banner	banner
gather	gather
salad	salad
celery	celery

6

Page 7

Words in Context
Write the missing spelling words.

Rest from the City

Challenge
Circle the other two-syllable words in the narrative with the /a/ and /e/ sounds.

Last (weekend,) my family stayed at a _____ **cabin** _____ in the woods. First, we all had to make an _____ **effort** _____ to _____ **gather** _____ up the things we needed to take. We loaded all our bags and a large _____ **package** _____ of supplies into the car. As we left the busy streets of the city crowded with _____ **traffic** _____, we (began to relax.)

Once we got into the country, we started looking for the _____ **address** _____ of our cabin on the mailboxes near the road. There was a moment of _____ **panic** _____ when we thought we were lost. Then, my dad saw the large red _____ **banner** _____ with the name of our (campground) written on it. We had finally arrived.

(After) we (unpacked) our things, we decided to go on a picnic. My mom packed a _____ **basket** _____ full of food and covered it with a large _____ **napkin** _____. My brother and I found a shady spot and spread out a _____ **blanket** _____ to sit on. We each had a ham _____ **sandwich** _____ with _____ **extra** _____ (lettuce) and tomato. We also had a mixed fruit _____ **salad** _____ and crisp stalks of _____ **celery** _____ spread with peanut butter. After we ate, we took a walk through the woods.

7

Page 8

Fun with Words
Unscramble the letters to make spelling words. Then, unscramble the letters that you circle to solve the riddle.

1. frictaf _____ **traffic** _____ Circle letters 2 and 6.
2. creyle _____ **celery** _____ Circle letters 3 and 6.
3. banic _____ **cabin** _____ Circle letter 1.
4. pankni _____ **napkin** _____ Circle letter 1.
5. takbes _____ **basket** _____ Circle letter 6.
6. daserds _____ **address** _____ Circle letters 4 and 5.
7. eakgcap _____ **package** _____ Circle letter 3.
8. trofef _____ **effort** _____ Circle letter 4.

What word in the dictionary is spelled incorrectly? _____ **incorrectly** _____

Words Across the Curriculum
Say each science word. Then, write the word.

1. cactus _____ **cactus** _____ 3. element _____ **element** _____
2. desert _____ **desert** _____ 4. predator _____ **predator** _____

Write the missing science words.

A _____ **desert** _____ is a hot, dry habitat that is home to many plants and animals. The dominant type of plant in this habitat is the _____ **cactus** _____. A common _____ **predator** _____ that eats small lizards and mice in this habitat is the rattlesnake. In the American Southwest, the _____ **element** _____ silver is found under the layers of sand and rock.

8

Page 9

Words in Writing
Write a narrative about something you like to do with your family. Use at least four words from the box.

Answers will vary.

sandwich	package	napkin	address	gather	cactus	desert
blanket	extra	panic	cabin	salad	element	predator
effort	traffic	basket	banner	celery		

Misspelled Words
Read the narrative and circle the seven misspelled words. Then, write the words correctly on the lines below.

I like to help my dad (gathar) vegetables from the garden. I pull carrots and (celary) from the ground and put them in a (baskit.) I also pick tomatoes, peppers, and other vegetables to use in a (saled) or on a (sandwitch.) Taking care of a garden is hard work, but it s worth the (exra) (effert.)

| **gather** | **basket** | **sandwich** | **effort** |
| **celery** | **salad** | **extra** | |

9

Answer Key

Say each word. Listen for the short **i**, **o**, and **u** sounds. Then, write the word.

Spelling Tip	The short **i**, **o**, and **u** sounds often come between two consonants. The symbol for the short **i** sound is /i/. The symbol for the short **o** sound is /o/. The symbol for the short **u** sound is /u/.

Spelling Words

exit	exit
bottom	bottom
electric	electric
suggest	suggest
polish	polish
until	until
river	river
closet	closet
victim	victim
inspect	inspect
possible	possible
distance	distance
umbrella	umbrella
window	window
finish	finish

10

Words in Context
Write the missing spelling words.

No Escape

Challenge
Circle the other two-syllable words in the story with the /i/, /o/, and /u/ sounds.

I was planning to meet my friends at the park by the __river__. Just as I was trying to make a quick __exit__ from the house, my mother appeared before me.

Have you forgotten what I told you? she asked. You re not to go anywhere __until__ you tidy up your room, she said, wagging her finger at me. I __suggest__ that you get it done now.

My heart sank, and I felt like a helpless __victim__. I knew it wasn t __possible__ to (invent) any excuses. I slowly trudged back to my room.

I ll be ready to __inspect__ your room when you __finish__ with it, I heard my mother call out from a __distance__.

I decided to surprise her by cleaning my room from top to __bottom__. I put my __umbrella__ and all my clothes away neatly in the __closet__. (dusted) the furniture and rubbed __polish__ on it. I ran the __electric__ vacuum cleaner. I even washed the __window__ and shined the mirror. Finally, my room was (spotless). My mother was going to be very (impressed).

11

Fun with Words
Alliteration is when a group of words have the same beginning sound. Use alliteration to write the spelling word that fits each sentence.

1. Clare cleaned her cluttered __closet__.
2. Will we wash the __window__ with water?
3. We huddled under our umbrella __until__ our uncle rescued us.
4. Ray rigged a rickety raft to ride the rapidly rising __river__.
5. Fred forgot to __finish__ feeding the fifty fish he found.
6. Eleven excited elephants escaped from the __exit__.
7. I ll __inspect__ the inside of the Inuit igloo.
8. Dozens of dentists drills droned in the __distance__.
9. Ben built a box in the __bottom__ of Bob s boat.

Words Across the Curriculum
Say each math word. Then, write the word.

1. multiple __multiple__   3. intersect __intersect__
2. prism __prism__   4. column __column__

Write the math word that completes each sentence.

1. A __column__ of data in a table is read from top to bottom.
2. Perpendicular lines __intersect__ one another.
3. The number 16 is a __multiple__ of 4.
4. A __prism__ is a solid shape that separates the colors of white light.

12

Words in Writing
Write a description of a chore that you do at home. Use at least two words from the box.

Answers will vary.

exit	suggest	river	inspect	umbrella	multiple	prism
bottom	polish	closet	possible	window	intersect	column
electric	until	victim	distance	finish		

Dictionary Practice
Write the words from the box in the columns where they belong. Some words belong in more than one column.

/i/ Sound

exit	inspect	distance
until	victim	river
polish	window	intersect
multiple	finish	prism
possible	electric	

/o/ Sound   **/u/ Sound**

bottom	until
polish	multiple
column	column
possible	umbrella
closet	suggest

13

Answer Key

Say each word. Listen to the beginning sounds. Then, write the word.

Spelling Tip	The letters **scr**, **squ**, **str**, and **thr** spell the beginning consonant sounds of some words.

Spelling Words

throne	throne
stretch	stretch
squirm	squirm
throw	throw
strap	strap
through	through
scream	scream
streak	streak
squeaky	squeaky
strength	strength
thrill	thrill
scrape	scrape
threat	threat
screw	screw
string	string

14

Words in Context
Write the missing spelling words.

Take a Deep Breath!

Challenge
Circle the other words with **scr**, **squ**, **str**, and **thr**.

Ride the Maximum Force roller coaster for the ____thrill____ of a lifetime! The moment you (squeeze) into a car and buckle your safety ____strap____, you ll begin to ____squirm____ nervously in your seat. The metal wheels of the cars will slowly ____scrape____ along the rails as you move upward. On the first hill, the ride will stop for a moment. You will feel like a king sitting on his ____throne____ as you look out on the grounds of the park that ____stretch____ out before you.

All of a sudden, the cars will jolt forward and nearly ____throw____ you out of your seat. The cars will ____streak____ along the track like lightning. As you seem to fly ____through____ the air, you will hang onto the safety bar with all of your ____strength____. You (throat) will be so dry with fright that you won t even be able to ____scream____. But don t worry there is no ____threat____ of danger. Although the cables sound ____squeaky____ and are no thicker than a ____string____, they re made of steel. Every latch, cable, and ____screw____ on the ride is secure.

15

Fun with Words
Write the spelling word that rhymes with each underlined word.

1. It s quite a ____thrill____ to run down the <u>hill</u>.
2. I started to ____scream____ when I had a bad <u>dream</u>.
3. When you pull on the ____string____, the bell will <u>ring</u>.
4. I touched the <u>worm</u>, and it started to ____squirm____.
5. Why did you ____scrape____ the skin off the <u>grape</u>?
6. The queen was <u>alone</u> as she sat on her ____throne____.
7. Why did you ____throw____ the ball in the <u>snow</u>?
8. Please fasten the ____strap____ across your <u>lap</u>.
9. The boys used all their ____strength____ to run the last <u>length</u>.
10. The old stairs are <u>creaky</u>, and they re also ____squeaky____.

Words Across the Curriculum
Say each science word. Then, write the word.

1. squid ____squid____   3. squash ____squash____
2. straw ____straw____   4. throat ____throat____

Write the science word that belongs with each group of words.

1. grass, wheat, hay, ____straw____
2. chin, ____throat____, neck, chest
3. potato, lettuce, tomato, ____squash____
4. octopus, ____squid____, jellyfish, sponge

16

Words in Writing
Write an ad for a ride or other attraction that you think is exciting. Use at least four words from the box.

Answers will vary.

throne	throw	scream	strength	threat	squid	straw
stretch	strap	streak	thrill	screw	squash	throat
squirm	through	squeaky	scrape	string		

Misspelled Words
Read the ad and circle the five misspelled words. Then, write the words correctly on the lines below.

Halloween is almost here, so be sure to visit the Haunted House. As you walk (thruogh) the dark (skweeky) house, you will have one scary (threll) after another. You will experience spooky sounds and sights that will stretch your imagination. Try not to (skream) as the giant worms (sqirm) all around you!

____through____   ____thrill____   ____squirm____
____squeaky____   ____scream____

17

Answer Key

Say each word. Listen for the /ch/ and /sh/ sounds. Then, write the word.

Spelling Tip	The /ch/ sound is often spelled **ch**. The /sh/ sound is often spelled **sh**.

Spelling Words

bunch	bunch
cheese	cheese
hunch	hunch
shift	shift
charge	charge
perch	perch
ranch	ranch
pinch	pinch
cherry	cherry
sheep	sheep
punch	punch
cheap	cheap
shelter	shelter
chief	chief
chance	chance

18

Words in Context
Write the missing spelling words.

Challenge
Circle the other words with /ch/ and /sh/.

Agriculture in California

California is the ____**chief**____ (agricultural) state. Crops are produced on a farm, while animals are raised on a ____**ranch**____. Orange, ____**cherry**____, and (peach) trees thrive in the hot days. The (chilly) nights give them a ____**chance**____ to recover from the heat.

During the harvest, every fruit picker works a long ____**shift**____ from morning to evening. Workers climb trees and ____**perch**____ on the lower (branches) (a) (reach) the fruit. Some workers ____**hunch**____ over (shrubs) to pick blueberries and raspberries. Others carefully pick (each) ____**bunch**____ of grapes from its vine. Later, other workers take the grapes to a covered ____**shelter**____ and ____**pinch**____ the grapes from their stems. Some of the grapes are made into juice and fruit ____**punch**____.

Cows and ____**sheep**____ are also raised in California, so the prices that the (ranchers) ____**charge**____ for dairy products, including milk and ____**cheese**____, are ____**cheap**____ there.

19

Fun with Words
Write the spelling word that answers the question What am I?

1. You need food, water and me to survive. What am I? ____**shelter**____

2. Horses and cattle live on me. What am I? ____**ranch**____

3. I can mean a change or a time period of work. What am I? ____**shift**____

4. I can be positive, negative, or neutral. What am I? ____**charge**____

5. I can be a group of bananas or grapes. What am I? ____**bunch**____

6. I am a leader of people or the main thing. What am I? ____**chief**____

7. I am a fruit and a popular flavor. What am I? ____**cherry**____

8. You might like me best when I m melted. What am I? ____**cheese**____

Words Across the Curriculum
Say each language arts word. Then, write the word.

1. chapter ____**chapter**____   3. publish ____**publish**____
2. research ____**research**____   4. English ____**English**____

Write the language arts word that fits each group of words.

1. edit, proofread, ____**publish**____
2. paragraph, page, ____**chapter**____
3. French, Spanish, ____**English**____
4. references, sources, ____**research**____

20

Words in Writing
Write a short report about some goods that are produced in your state. Use at least four words from the box.

____
____
____
____   Answers will vary.

bunch	shift	ranch	sheep	shelter	chapter	research
cheese	charge	pinch	punch	chief	publish	English
hunch	perch	cherry	cheap	chance		

Misspelled Words
Read the paragraph from a report. Circle the five misspelled words. Then, write the words correctly on the lines below.

I did some (researsh) about some foods and animals that are raised on farms in Wisconsin. Cows, hogs, and (sheap) make up most of the livestock raised in the state. A huge amount of milk (chease) and other dairy products are produced there, so these products are fairl (cheep) for the people of this state. I was surprised to find that Wisconsin farmers grow a large number of (chery) trees. However, apples are their chief fruit crop.

____**research**____   ____**cheese**____   ____**cherry**____
____**sheep**____   ____**cheap**____

21

Answer Key

Say each word. Listen to the sound of each consonant diagraph and notice which letter is silent. Then, write the word.

Spelling Tip	The consonant diagraphs **gn**, **mb**, **tch**, and **wr** each have a silent letter. In the consonant diagraph **gn**, the **g** is silent. In the consonant diagraph **mb**, the **b** is silent. In the consonant diagraph **tch**, the **t** is silent. In the consonant blend **wr**, the **w** is silent.

Spelling Words

fetch	fetch
wren	wren
sketch	sketch
design	design
wreck	wreck
comb	comb
twitch	twitch
wrinkle	wrinkle
ditch	ditch
patch	patch
limb	limb
align	align
wrench	wrench
clutch	clutch
snatch	snatch

22

Words in Context
Write the missing spelling words.

Challenge
Circle the other words with **gn**, **mb**, **tch**, and **wr**.

Building a Birdhouse

Our art class had an interesting (assignment.) We each had to ____design____ a birdhouse. I began by making a ____sketch____. I didn't have a ruler, so I used the edge of my ____comb____ to draw straight lines. When I was finished, I began to ____fetch____ the materials I needed to build my birdhouse.

I took some wood, nails, and my drawing out to a tree in my backyard. Then, I had to ____clutch____ my saw, a hammer, and a ____wrench____ all at once and carry them to the tree. There, I saw my cat try to ____snatch____ my drawing. I knew that he was trying to ____wreck____ my plan to build a safe place for birds. I chased him into a ____ditch____ at the end of the yard. Then, I smoothed out the ____wrinkle____ in my drawing. I carved a (notch) on a ____limb____ of the tree to mark the place for my birdhouse. As I built it, I tried to ____align____ all the pieces of wood.

Now, a small brown ____wren____ with a ____patch____ of black on her throat often visits my birdhouse. She likes to (watch) my cat, who can only stare back at her and ____twitch____ his whiskers. He can t (climb) the tree.

23

Fun with Words
Write the spelling word that fits each sentence and has a consonant diagraph that sounds the same as the underlined letters.

1. Will you please ____fetch____ the ma<u>tch</u>es from the hu<u>tch</u>?
2. Rachel will i<u>r</u>on the ____wrinkle____ in her <u>r</u>ed d<u>r</u>ess.
3. Can you ____design____ a si<u>gn</u> to sell bolo<u>gn</u>a?
4. The ca<u>tch</u>er tried to ____snatch____ the ball before it rolled into the di<u>tch</u>.
5. The ____wrench____ is the <u>wr</u>ong tool to use to <u>r</u>epair the <u>r</u>ake.
6. Please ____align____ the twi<u>ne</u> with the stem of the vi<u>ne</u>.
7. Did you atta<u>ch</u> a ____patch____ on your scra<u>tch</u>?
8. The tiny b<u>r</u>own ____wren____ perched on the <u>wr</u>eath.

Words Across the Curriculum
Say each social studies word. Then, write the word.

1. wreath	wreath	3. lasagna	lasagna
2. tomb	tomb	4. hitch	hitch

Write the social studies word that completes each sentence.

1. ____Lasagna____ is an Italian dish made with pasta, meat, and cheese.
2. Some people hang a ____wreath____ on the door during holidays.
3. Each pyramid in Egypt is the ____tomb____ of an ancient king or queen.
4. In the Old West, people used to ____hitch____ their horses to posts outside of stores.

24

Words in Writing
Write directions telling how to make or fix something. Use at least four words from the box.

Answers will vary.

fetch	design	twitch	patch	wrench	wreath	tomb
wren	wreck	wrinkle	limb	clutch	lasagna	hitch
sketch	comb	ditch	align	snatch		

Dictionary Practice
Write the words from the box in alphabetical order. For some words, you will have to look at the third or fourth letter.

1.	align	8.	lasagna	15.	wreath
2.	clutch	9.	limb	16.	wreck
3.	comb	10.	patch	17.	wren
4.	design	11.	sketch	18.	wrench
5.	ditch	12.	snatch	19.	wrinkle
6.	fetch	13.	tomb		
7.	hitch	14.	twitch		

25

Answer Key

Write the spelling word that fits with each group of words.

1. lettuce, radish, carrot, _____celery_____
2. mattress, pillow, sheets, _____blanket_____
3. peach, plum, apricot, _____cherry_____
4. bolt, nut, nail, _____screw_____
5. rope, cord, twine, _____string_____
6. sparrow, robin, finch, _____wren_____
7. milk, yogurt, butter, _____cheese_____
8. soup, salad, chips, _____sandwich_____
9. brook, creek, stream, _____river_____
10. hand, palm, thumb, _____finger_____

Write the spelling word that is a synonym for each word below.

11. shine _____polish_____
12. propose _____suggest_____
13. excitement _____thrill_____
14. ruin _____wreck_____
15. flag _____banner_____
16. end _____finish_____

26

Write the spelling word that means the same as each word below.

17. collect _____gather_____
18. shriek _____scream_____
19. toss _____throw_____
20. grab _____snatch_____
21. branch _____limb_____
22. wriggle _____squirm_____

Write the spelling word that completes each sentence.

23. Did you pack the food in the picnic _____basket_____?
24. The girls hung their coats in the _____closet_____.
25. The wheels of the old bike sound _____squeaky_____.
26. I taught my dog to _____fetch_____ the newspaper.
27. I bought a _____bunch_____ of ripe bananas.
28. Dad tightened the bolt on my bike with a _____wrench_____.
29. I like the geometric _____design_____ on that quilt.
30. Did you get _____extra_____ credit for your report?

27

Say each word. Listen for the long **a** sound. Then, write the word.

Spelling Tip	The long **a** sound can be spelled **a**, **a-consanant-e**, **ai**, **ay**, **ea**, and **eigh**. The symbol for the long **a** sound is /ā/.

Spelling Words

steak	steak
plain	plain
agent	agent
weight	weight
amaze	amaze
danger	danger
brain	brain
bacon	bacon
brave	brave
escape	escape
paper	paper
neighbor	neighbor
trace	trace
cable	cable
behave	behave

28

Words in Context
Write the missing spelling words.

A Tall, Tall Tale

Challenge
Circle the other words with the /ā/ sound.

My dog Albert is incredible. The things he can do would truly _____amaze_____ you. First of all, he uses his _____brain_____ to think like a human. He doesn t _____behave_____ like a dog at all. Albert likes to (lay) on the couch and watch cooking programs on _____cable_____ TV. He writes down the recipes on notebook _____paper_____. Last night, Albert invited our next-door _____neighbor_____ over for dinner. Albert (made) grilled _____steak_____, (baked) (potatoes) and a salad topped with cheese and _____bacon_____.

Albert is much more than a (great) cook. He is also a very _____great_____ dog who tracks criminals in his (spare) time. He once helped a secret _____agent_____ catch an international thief. Albert (trailed) the thief along a beach in (Maine.) The thief thought that Albert was just a _____plain_____, ordinary dog. Thinking that he was in no _____danger_____ of being caught, the thief broke into a beach house and stole some jewels. He thought he would _____escape_____ from the house without leaving a _____trace_____ of evidence. But Albert threw all the _____weight_____ of his body at the thief and knocked him down. Then, he used his cell phone to call for backup.

29

Answer Key

Page 30

Fun with Words

Write the spelling word that completes each comparison.

1. *Chalk* is to *board* as *pen* is to _____paper_____.
2. *Inches* is to *height* as *pounds* is to _____weight_____.
3. *Public* is to *police* as *secret* is to _____agent_____.
4. *Battery* is to *cell phone* as _____cable_____ is to *television*.
5. *Breathe* is to *lungs* as *think* is to _____brain_____.
6. *Steak* is to *potatoes* as _____bacon_____ is to *eggs*.
7. *Amazing* is to *unusual* as *ordinary* is to _____plain_____.
8. *Afraid* is to *scared* as *fearless* is to _____brave_____.
9. *Thrill* is to *boredom* as *safety* is to _____danger_____.
10. *Unfriendly* is to *enemy* as *friendly* is to _____neighbor_____.

Words Across the Curriculum

Say each math word. Then, write the word.

1. scale _____scale_____
3. eighth _____eighth_____
2. radius _____radius_____
4. table _____table_____

Write the math word that fits each group of words.

1. row, column, data, _____table_____
2. area, diameter, circumference, _____radius_____
3. fifth, sixth, seventh, _____eighth_____
4. balance, spring, weigh, _____scale_____

30

Page 31

Words in Writing

Write a tall tale using made-up characters and exaggeration. Use at least four words from the box.

Answers will vary.

steak	weight	brain	escape	trace	scale	radius
plain	amaze	bacon	paper	cable	eighth	table
agent	danger	brave	neighbor	behave		

Dictionary Practice

Read the dictionary entries below. Then, read the example sentences. Write the part of speech and the number of the definition of the underlined words.

cable (kā« bel) *n.* 1. a strong, thick cord. 2. A bundle of wires enclosed in a protective covering and used to carry an electric current. *adj.* 1. Transmitted by cable TV. *v.* 1. To transmit a message.

plain (plān) *adj.* 1. Clearly seen or heard. 2. Obvious; clearly understood. 3. Without decoration. 4. ordinary. *n.* 1. An area of level land.

1. The judge made it <u>plain</u> that he did not agree. _____adjective, 2_____
2. Suspension bridges are held up by steel <u>cables</u>. _____noun, 1_____
3. The woman wore a <u>plain</u> black raincoat. _____adjective, 3_____
4. I like to watch comedy shows on <u>cable</u> TV. _____adjective, 1_____

31

Page 32

Say each word. Listen for the long **e** sound. Then, write the word.

| **Spelling Tip** | The long **e** sound can be spelled **e**, **ee**, **ea**, **ie**, **y**, and **ey**. The symbol for the long **e** sound is /ē/. |

Spelling Words

steam	steam
sweet	sweet
honey	honey
shield	shield
treat	treat
screech	screech
least	least
beetle	beetle
reason	reason
breathe	breathe
field	field
beast	beast
valley	valley
species	species
monkey	monkey

32

Page 33

Words in Context

Write the missing spelling words.

Challenge

Circle the other words in the report with the /ē/ sound.

Life in a Rain Forest

Tropical rain forests are the most diverse (ecosystems) on Earth. More than half of all plant and animal _____species_____ live in rain forests, which (receive) at _____least_____ 50 inches of rain per year. Sometimes, the rain is so warm that water droplets rise back into the air in the form of _____steam_____. Rain forest (trees) give off oxygen that animals (need) to _____breathe_____. The (trees) are often clustered around a sloping river _____valley_____.

Most rain forest (trees) have (leafy) branches that grow only at the top. (These) branches, called the (canopy), _____shield_____ the forest floor from sunlight. From above, the (canopy) looks like a huge (green) _____field_____.

All kinds of nuts and tropical fruits that are as _____sweet_____ as _____honey_____ grow in the (canopy). For this _____reason_____, most rain forest animals live in the (canopy). There, it is common to (see) a _____monkey_____ or two swinging from branch to branch as they _____screech_____ loudly at one another and search for fruit, nuts, or a special _____treat_____, such as a cricket or a plump _____beetle_____. A strange _____beast_____, called a *sloth*, also lives in the (canopy).

33

Answer Key

Fun with Words

Circle the word in each sentence that is contained in the underlined spelling word. There can be more than one possible answer.

1. The impish <u>monkey</u> hid the (key) to his cage.
2. Let s (eat) (a) cookie for (a) (treat).
3. (The) air that we <u>breathe</u> contains oxygen.
4. (One) swarm of bees can produce a lot of <u>honey</u>.
5. The driver needs to take at <u>least</u> one more turn before he heads (east).
6. A (team) of scientists designed (a) new <u>steam</u> engine.
7. The student had (a) good <u>reason</u> for being late.
8. A black <u>beetle</u> is nibbling on the (beet).
9. (We) like to eat <u>sweet</u> berries.
10. At the end of the (alley) you can see the distant <u>valley</u>.

Words Across the Curriculum

Say each math word. Then, write the word.

1. mean   **mean**   3. capacity   **capacity**
2. degree   **degree**   4. median   **median**

Write each math word next to its definition.

1. a unit used to measure temperature   **degree**
2. the middle number in a group of numbers arranged from least to greatest   **median**
3. the amount of liquid that a container can hold   **capacity**
4. the average of a group of numbers   **mean**

34

Words in Writing

Write a short report about a rain forest animal. Use at least four words from the box.

_____

_____

Answers will vary.

_____

_____

steam	shield	least	breathe	valley	mean	degree
reason	treat	beetle	field	species	capacity	median
honey	screech	sweet	beast	monkey		

Misspelled Words

Read the paragraph. Circle the six misspelled words. Then, write the words correctly on the lines below.

Several different (speces) of monkeys live in tropical rain forests. Most rain forest monkeys are very social, like humans. They chatter with one another and (screach) loudly to warn other monkeys when a dangerous (beest) is nearby. Monkeys eat leaves, (sweate) fruits, flowers, seeds, and insects. A favorite treat of some monkeys is fresh (honee) or a plump (beatle).

species   **beast**   **honey**

screech   **sweet**   **beetle**

35

Say each word. Listen for the long **i** sound. Then, write the word.

Spelling Tip	The long **i** sound can be spelled **i**, **i-consonant-e**, **igh**, and **y**. The symbol for the long **i** sound is /ī/.

Spelling Words

price	**price**
mild	**mild**
supply	**supply**
fight	**fight**
invite	**invite**
surprise	**surprise**
private	**private**
divide	**divide**
slight	**slight**
lightning	**lightning**
quite	**quite**
bicycle	**bicycle**
decide	**decide**
library	**library**
drive	**drive**

36

Words in Context

Write the missing spelling words.

It s a Party!

Challenge

Circle the other words in the letter with the /ī/ sound.

Dear (Mike),

(I m) (writing) to **invite** you to a **surprise** party for Casey. The party is next Saturday at (Highland) Park, which is (right) next to the public **library**. The weather should be sunny and **mild**, with only a **slight** chance of rain and **lightning**. (Kristi) and (I) reserved the **private** shelter near the pond. The party starts at (five) o clock.

We will have a large **supply** of food and soda. After we eat, we can **divide** into two teams and play baseball. (I) bought **quite** a few water balloons for a very low **price**, so we can also have a water-balloon **fight**. We can **decide** later what other games to play.

(I) hope you can come to the party. (I) think it will be really (exciting)! You could (ride) your **bicycle** to my house, and then my dad can **drive** us both to the park. Let me know soon.

Your friend,
(Robbie)

37

Spectrum Spelling
Grade 4

Answer Key

Page 38

Fun with Words
Write the spelling word that completes each quote.

1. "Life is like riding a ___bicycle___. You don't fall off unless you stop pedaling." —Claude Pepper

2. "When elephants ___fight___, it is the grass that suffers." —African proverb

3. "If you must play, ___decide___ upon three things at the start: the rules of the game, the stakes, and the quitting time." —Chinese proverb

4. A wizard is never late, Frodo Baggins. Nor is he early. He will always ___arrive___ precisely when he means to." —Gandalf, from *The Lord of the Rings*

5. "___Divide___ and rule, unite and lead." —Johann Wolfgang von Goethe

6. "When you reach for the stars you may not ___quite___ get one, but you won't come up with a handful of mud either." —Leo Burnett

Words Across the Curriculum
Say each science word. Then, write the word.

1. tide ___tide___   3. hydrogen ___hydrogen___
2. biome ___biome___   4. vitamin ___vitamin___

Write the science word that completes each sentence.

1. The Sun is made up of mostly helium and ___hydrogen___.
2. A ___vitamin___ is a chemical compound that human bodies need.
3. A ___tide___ is the rise and fall of surface water in the ocean.
4. A desert is a ___biome___ that receives very little rain.

38

Page 39

Words in Writing
Write a letter to a friend. Use at least four words from the box.

Answers will vary.

price	fight	private	lightning	decide	tide	biome
mild	invite	divide	quite	library	hydrogen	vitamin
supply	surprise	slight	bicycle	drive		

Dictionary Practice
Divide the words below into syllables using hyphens. Use a dictionary if you need help.

1. invite ___in-vite___   6. hydrogen ___hy-dro-gen___
2. biome ___bi-ome___   7. lightning ___light-ning___
3. supply ___sup-ply___   8. surprise ___sur-prise___
4. divide ___di-vide___   9. library ___li-brar-y___
5. private ___pri-vate___   10. bicycle ___bi-cy-cle___

39

Page 40

Say each word. Listen for the long **o** sound. Then, write the word.

Spelling Tip
The long **o** sound can be spelled **o**, **o-consonant-e**, **oa**, **ough**, and **ow**. The symbol for the long **o** sound is /ō/.

Spelling Words

over	over
broke	broke
motion	motion
below	below
choke	choke
stolen	stolen
noble	noble
moment	moment
swallow	swallow
notice	notice
spoke	spoke
croak	croak
propose	propose
hollow	hollow
although	although

40

Page 41

Words in Context
Write the missing spelling words.

Challenge
Circle the other words in the fable with the /ō/ sound.

The Fox and the Crow

A black (crow) sat on a limb of a ___hollow___ tree. He was (holding) a piece of cheese in his beak. The (crow) did not ___swallow___ the cheese. Instead, he held it in his beak (so) that the fox sitting ___below___ the tree would ___notice___ it. The fox stared up at the (crow) for a ___moment___. Then, he ___broke___ the silence.

My, what a handsome and ___noble___ bird you are, said the sly fox. Too bad your voice is just an ugly ___croak___. The (crow) became very angry. ___Although___ he tried to ___choke___ back his words, he couldn t remain quiet.

That s not true! I have a beautiful voice, the (crow) (boasted). As soon as he ___spoke___, the cheese fell from his beak. With a single quick ___motion___, the fox grabbed the cheese. The (crow) (groaned) in despair as he watched the fox dine on the ___stolen___ cheese.

Thank you, said the fox, running his tongue ___over___ his lips. May I ___propose___ a word of advice? Eating is more important than pride.

41

Page 42

Fun with Words

Clichés are common figures of speech that people use over and over again. Write the spelling word that completes each cliché.

1. This is the straw that **broke** the camel's back.

2. There's no point crying **over** spilled milk.

3. I decided to go shopping on the spur of the **moment**.

4. I was so sad that I had to **choke** back my tears.

5. The lion is a **noble** beast that's known as the king of the jungle.

6. We couldn't understand her, because she **spoke** in riddles.

7. That insult was really hard to **swallow**.

8. **Although** the thief looks honest, he lies like a rug.

Words Across the Curriculum

Say each science word. Then, write the word.

1. motor **motor**
2. ocean **ocean**
3. rotate **rotate**
4. proton **proton**

Write the science word that completes each sentence.

1. It takes Earth 24 hours to **rotate** on its axis.

2. An electric **motor** changes electricity into mechanical energy.

3. The Pacific is the largest **ocean** on Earth.

4. A **proton** has a positive charge.

42

Page 43

Words in Writing

A fable is a short story that teaches a lesson about life. It includes a sentence or two at the end that tells what the lesson is. Write an existing fable in your own words, or make up a new one. Use at least four words from the box.

Answers will vary.

over	below	noble	notice	propose	motor	ocean
broke	choke	moment	spoke	hollow	rotate	proton
motion	stolen	swallow	croak	although		

Misspelled Words

Read the first paragraph of the fable. Circle the five misspelled words. Then, write the words correctly on the lines below.

A town mouse invited his country cousin over for dinner. The two mice were enjoying the scraps left on the dining table from a (noable) feast. They didn't (noetice) the (mosion) of the hungry cat entering the room, although they did hear a most frightening noise: a sound like the purring of a (motore). The two mice froze and looked into the darkness (beloe) the table.

noble   motion   below
notice   motor

43

Page 44

Say each word. Listen for the long **u** and /oo/ sound. Then, write the word.

| **Spelling Tip** | The long **u** sound can be spelled **o-consonant-e, u, ue, iew, u-consonant-e**. The symbol for the long **u** sound is /ū/. The **oo** sound can be spelled **ew, u-consonant-e, oo,** and **ue**. The symbol for the /oo/ sound is / /. |

Spelling Words

proof	**proof**
duty	**duty**
stew	**stew**
issue	**issue**
review	**review**
smooth	**smooth**
value	**value**
whose	**whose**
troop	**troop**
truce	**truce**
regular	**regular**
include	**include**
argue	**argue**
usually	**usually**
continue	**continue**

44

Page 45

Words in Context

Write the missing spelling words.

Please Join Our Group

| **Challenge** |
| Circle the other words with the /ū/ or / / sounds. |

Would (you) like to join a (group) of fun people? If so, we would like to **include** (you) as a member of our scouting **troop**. Our **regular** meetings are on the first (Tuesday) of each month.

At our meetings, we **usually** make plans for (future) activities. We also collect (dues), which we (use) to pay for our activities. We **review** any other **issue** that scout members want to discuss. We try not to **argue** about these matters or (lose) our tempers. Instead, we talk calmly and try to **smooth** out any disagreements. We (truly) **value** every person's opinion. If we can't agree on something, we call a **truce**. Then, we **continue** the discussion at the next meeting.

Our scouts have a strong sense of **duty** to our (community.) This year, we had a yard sale to raise money for a family **whose** house was damaged by a fire. We also made a (huge) patch of beef **stew** for the homeless center. These activities are **proof** of our commitment to our (community.)

45

Answer Key

Fun with Words

Unscramble the letters to make spelling words. Then, unscramble the letters that you circle to solve the riddle.

1. grealru _____regular_____ Circle letter 5.
2. sweho _____whose_____ Circle letter 5.
3. dunlice _____include_____ Circle letter 3.
4. wivere _____review_____ Circle letter 4.
5. turfeu _____future_____ Circle letter 6.
6. shomot _____smooth_____ Circle letter 1.
7. notunice _____continue_____ Circle letter 3.

What is so fragile that even saying its name can break it? _____silence_____

Words Across the Curriculum

Say each art word. Then, write the word.

1. music _____music_____   3. flute _____flute_____
2. unity _____unity_____   4. statue _____statue_____

Write the art word that fits with each group of words.

1. variety, harmony, balance, _____unity_____
2. piano, trumpet, guitar, _____flute_____
3. tune, melody, song, _____music_____
4. painting, drawing, pottery, _____statue_____

46

Words in Writing

Write a flyer that persuades people to join a club or other group. Use at least four words from the box.

_____
_____
_____
_____

Answers will vary.

_____
_____

proof	issue	value	truce	argue	music	unity
duty	review	whose	regular	usually	flute	statue
stew	smooth	troop	include	continue		

Dictionary Practice

Write the number of syllables in each word below.

1. issue _____2_____   6. regular _____3_____
2. unity _____3_____   7. statue _____2_____
3. smooth _____1_____   8. include _____2_____
4. continue _____3_____ 9. review _____2_____
5. duty _____2_____   10. usually _____4_____

47

Write the spelling word that is an antonym of each word below.

1. safety _____danger_____
2. unite _____divide_____
3. solid _____hollow_____
4. above _____below_____
5. public _____private_____
6. greatest _____least_____
7. sour _____sweet_____
8. rarely _____usually_____
9. fixed _____broke_____
10. rough _____smooth_____
11. bought _____stolen_____

Write the spelling word that belongs with each group of words.

12. juice, eggs, toast, _____bacon_____
13. meadow, pasture, grassland, _____field_____
14. skateboard, wagon, scooter, _____bicycle_____
15. string, cord, rope, _____cable_____
16. offer, suggest, advise, _____propose_____

48

Write the spelling word that is a synonym of each word below.

17. simple _____plain_____
18. movement _____motion_____
19. evidence _____proof_____
20. protect _____shield_____
21. purpose _____reason_____
22. cost _____price_____
23. very _____quite_____
24. battle _____fight_____

Write the spelling word that rhymes with each pair of words below.

25. beach, teach, _____screech_____
26. scoop, group, _____troop_____
27. lose, choose, _____whose_____
28. wake, break, _____steak_____
29. chunky, junky, _____monkey_____
30. rally, tally, _____valley_____
31. dream, cream, _____steam_____
32. money, funny, _____honey_____

49

Answer Key

Say each word. Listen for the / r/ sound. Then, write the word.

Spelling Tip	The / r/ sound can be spelled or, ore, and our.

Spelling Words

port	port
force	force
source	source
support	support
chore	chore
report	report
before	before
fort	fort
course	course
order	order
explore	explore
record	record
border	border
landform	landform
history	history

50

Words in Context
Write the missing spelling words.

Challenge
Circle the other words in the report with the / r/ sound.

A Famous Expedition

In 1804, Merriwether Lewis and William Clark began one of the most (important) journeys in American __history__. By the __order__ of President Thomas Jefferson, they left St. Louis to __explore__ the western United States. The year __before__, the president had bought this (territory) from the French. The (territory) included the __port__ city of New (Orleans) It extended the western __border__ of the United States from the Mississippi River to the Pacific Ocean.

Lewis and Clark began their journey (aboard) a keelboat on the Missouri River and followed the river to its __source__. They took 50 men with them (for) protection and __support__. They also built a __fort__. As the __force__ of the river carried them along, Clark spent most of his time charting their __course__ and making maps. He was very careful not to make an error in his calculations. Lewis s main __chore__ was to __record__ his (observations) of the strange new animals, plants, and __landform__ that he saw. Lewis would later __report__ this (information) to the president.

51

Fun with Words
Use the letters of each spelling word below to make at least three four-letter words. **Answers will vary. Possible answers.**

1. landform ___land, form, from, roam, foal___
2. course ___our, ours, core, sore, sour, rose, sure___
3. support ___port, sport, spot, stop, pour___
4. record ___cord, rode, code, core, order___
5. before ___robe, bore, beef, reef, free___
6. history ___stir, story, short, shirt, this___

7. Two of the spelling words have all of the same letters. The only difference is that two of the letters are reversed. Which words are they?
___source, course___

Words Across the Curriculum
Say each social studies word. Then, write the word.

1. court ___court___   3. uniform ___uniform___
2. afford ___afford___   4. export ___export___

Write the social studies word that completes each sentence.

1. The United States and Canada ___export___ many goods.
2. If you can t ___afford___ to buy something you want right away, you can wait until you save enough money.
3. A trial is held in a ___court___.
4. A police officer wears a ___uniform___ so that people can identify him or her.

52

Words in Writing
If you could live in any place at any time in history, where would it be? Write about this time and place. Use at least four words from the box.

Answers will vary.

port	support	before	order	border	court	afford
force	chore	fort	explore	landform	uniform	export
source	report	course	record	history		

Misspelled Words
Read the description. Circle the five misspelled words. Then, write the words correctly on the lines below.

If I could go back in history, I d like to live about 100 years ago. I would live on a tropical island in the day (befor) many tourists visited it. I would (explour) every beach and (landforme) d keep a journal to (recorde) all the interesting things I saw. I would also sail on a boat beyond the (boreder) of the land.

___before___   ___landform___   ___border___
___explore___   ___record___

53

Page 54

Say each word. Listen for the / r/ sound. Then, write the word.

Spelling Tip	The / r / sound can be spelled **er, ear, ir, or,** and **ur.**

Spelling Words

curve	curve
heard	heard
worry	worry
further	further
perfect	perfect
worth	worth
return	return
shirt	shirt
hurry	hurry
surge	surge
expert	expert
search	search
purpose	purpose
certain	certain
thirsty	thirsty

54

Page 55

Words in Context
Write the missing spelling words.

Earning a Comeback

This morning was my first soccer game of the season, but I overslept. I had to ___search___ through my closet for my gear and ___hurry___ to the field as quickly as I could. I was ___certain___ that I d be late, but it turned out that there was no need to ___worry___. The game hadn t started yet.

I took off my ___shirt___ and put on my jersey. Then, I ___heard___ the referee blow his whistle, so I joined my team on the field. During the first half of the game, the opposing team dominated us. Our players pursued the ball without any real ___purpose___. At halftime, we were discouraged, hot, and ___thirsty___. We did not think it was ___worth___ the effort to ___return___ to the field to face ___further___ embarrassment.

Somehow, our coach managed to encourage us. He is an ___expert___ at making us focus on doing our best. We came back in the second half with a ___surge___ of energy. With the score tied near the end of the game, our best striker scored a ___perfect___ goal. He faked around his defender and was able to ___curve___ the ball into the top of the goal.

55

Page 56

Fun with Words
Use the clues to complete the puzzle with spelling words.

Across
1. look for
3. needing water
4. just right
5. be troubled about
6. master or specialist

Down
1. a burst
2. sure
4. reason

Crossword answers:
- 1 Across: search
- 4 Across: perfect
- 3 Across: thirsty
- 5 Across: worry
- 6 Across: expert
- 1 Down: surge
- 2 Down: certain
- 4 Down: purpose

Words Across the Curriculum
Say each science word. Then, write the word.

1. germ ___germ___   3. current ___current___
2. Earth ___Earth___   4. pearl ___pearl___

Write the science word that completes each sentence.

1. A ___current___ can flow deep beneath the surface of the ocean.
2. The moon revolves around ___Earth___.
3. A ___germ___ can be seen only with a microscope.
4. A ___pearl___ is a gem formed inside of an oyster.

56

Page 57

Words in Writing
Describe a sports event that you watched or participated in. Use at least four words from the box.

Answers will vary.

curve	further	return	surge	purpose	germ	Earth
heard	perfect	shirt	expert	certain	current	pearl
worry	worth	hurry	search	thirsty		

Dictionary Practice
Circle the correct pronunciation for the words below. Use a dictionary if you need help.

1. pearl   perl   (p rl)   p r el
2. curve   c rve   (k rv)   kerv
3. perfect   p rf« ect   per« fek   (p r« fikt)
4. further   fur« thur   (f r« ther)   ferth« er
5. thirsty   th rs« tl   thir« ste   (th r« ste)
6. heard   herd   h red   (h rd)
7. surge   surg   c rj   (s rj)

57

Answer Key

Page 58

Say each word. Listen for the /ə/ sound in the final syllable. Then, write the word.

Spelling Tip	The /ə/ sound can be spelled **a**, **e**, and **o**. The /ə/ sound is common in unstressed syllables.

Spelling Words

model	model
royal	royal
cotton	cotton
central	central
custom	custom
flavor	flavor
towel	towel
happen	happen
local	local
lemon	lemon
jewel	jewel
capital	capital
travel	travel
normal	normal
natural	natural

58

Page 59

Words in Context
Write the missing spelling words.

An Unusual Shopping Trip

If you ever __happen__ to __travel__ to Egypt, be sure to visit the famous marketplace in the middle of Cairo, the __capital__ city. The marketplace has many ancient walls and buildings, including a __royal__ palace. This marketplace is nothing like a __normal__ mall in the United States.

Inside the __central__ part of the marketplace, there is a maze of shops that sell almost any item that you can imagine. You can find an inexpensive __model__ of a famous piece of Egyptian art or a copy of a valuable __jewel__. You also can find a carpet, __towel__, or other piece of cloth made of fine wool or __cotton__.

Outside the marketplace, many __local__ farmers set up stalls with fruits, vegetables, and other __natural__ products, which they unload each day from their wagons. You can almost taste the bitter __flavor__ of a juicy __lemon__ or an exotic spice. It is a __custom__ in Egypt to bargain with the shopkeepers over their prices.

59

Page 60

Fun with Words
The letters in one or two words in each sentence can be rearranged to form a spelling word. Circle the words and then rearrange the letters to make the spelling word.

1. I will (not) (sit) on that (cot). __cotton__
2. The (lunar) spaceship landed on the moon (at) noon. __natural__
3. My dad (lent) his (car) to his barber. __central__
4. Would you like a ripe, juicy (melon)? __lemon__
5. Did you (lay) your gloves down (or) did you lose them? __royal__
6. (We) bought (a lot) of apples today. __towel__
7. The (old) man gave (me) some wise advice. __model__
8. I did a (sum) while I lay on the (cot). __custom__

Words Across the Curriculum
Say each science word. Then, write the word.

1. metal __metal__ 3. carbon __carbon__
2. organ __organ__ 4. water __waer__

1. The __organ__ that pumps blood in an animal s body is the heart.
2. __Water__ is a mixture of hydrogen and oxygen.
3. A __metal__ is usually a hard, solid, shiny substance.
4. __Carbon__ is an element found in the remains of all living things.

60

Page 61

Words in Writing
Describe a tradition in your family.
Use at least four words from the box.

Answers will vary.

model	central	towel	lemon	travel	metal	organ
royal	custom	happen	jewel	normal	carbon	water
cotton	capital	local	flavor	natural		

Misspelled Words
Read the description. Circle the five misspelled words. Then, write the words correctly on the lines below.

My grandmother is from the (centrel) part of Greece. She isn t able to (traval) here very often, but she still follows many Greek customs. She makes Greek food using (naturel) ingredients that she buys from a local farm market. She uses (lemen) juice to add a tar (flaver) to many of the dishes she makes.

__central__   __natural__   __flavor__
__travel__   __lemon__

61

Answer Key

Write the spelling word that is an antonym of each word below.

1. closer   further
2. after   before
3. unsure   certain
4. game   chore
5. unusual   normal
6. leave   return

Write the spelling word that is a synonym of each word below.

7. goal   purpose
8. tradition   custom
9. command   order
10. arch   curve
11. taste   flavor
12. occur   happen
13. mistake   error
14. edge   border
15. value   worth

62

Write the spelling word that belongs with each group of words.

16. mountain, desert, volcano,   landform
17. aching, tired, hungry,   thirsty
18. pants, sweater, vest,   shirt
19. king, queen, prince,   royal
20. orange, grapefruit, lime,   lemon
21. velvet, wool, silk,   cotton
22. diamond, ruby, emerald,   jewel
23. seek, hunt, pursue,   search
24. journey, trip, visit,   travel
25. robe, washcloth, sponge,   towel
26. inform, notify, broadcast   report
27. origin, root, beginning,   source
28. pro, master, specialist   expert
29. help, aid, assistance,   support
30. power, strength, might,   force

63

Say each word. Notice how the order of the **s** and the apostrophe shows whether the word is singular or plural. Then, write the word.

| Spelling Tip | **Possessive nouns** are words that show ownership. When a noun shows that one person or thing owns something, the noun ends with **s**. Usually, when a noun shows that more than one person or thing owns something, the noun ends with **s**. |

Spelling Words

baby s	baby s
mother s	mother s
brothers	brothers
officer s	officer s
friend s	friend s
sister s	sister s
children s	children s
family s	family s
everyone s	everyone s
hamster s	hamster s
friends	friends
father s	father s
grandmothers	grandmothers
customers	customers
families	families

64

Words in Context
Write the missing spelling words.

Everything Not Being Used Must Go!

This summer, the people on my block had a big yard sale. The sale was held in my ____family s____ yard. This was my ____mother s____ idea. At first, she just wanted to get rid of my youngest ____sister s____ old dresses and coats. Then, she decided that both of my ____brothers____ old baseball equipment had to go, too. She began searching through ____everyone s____ closets and drawers to see what she could get rid of. She even went through my ____father s____ office to find things that he didn t use anymore.

My mother offered to help clear out some of her ____friends____ houses, too. Soon, our yard was filled with other ____families____ old and unused items. There was a ____baby s____ crib, a ____hamster s____ cage, an old police ____officer s____ uniform, and all kinds of ____children s____ toys and clothes. My best ____friend s____ mother brought over a box full of both of her ____grandmothers____ old-fashioned dresses. When the sale was over, we had collected more than $200 of our ____customers____ money.

65

Page 66

Fun with Words

Write the spelling word that explains the relationship described in each sentence.

1. My mother s sons bikes are my **brothers** bikes.
2. My parents mothers coats are my **grandmothers** coats.
3. My mother s daughter s desk is my **sister s** desk.
4. My grandfather s only son s car is my **father s** car.
5. My buddy s mother is my **friend s** mother.
6. My aunt s only sister s dog is my **mother s** dog.
7. My parents **children s** toys are my brother s and sister s toys.
8. My parents and their children s house is my **family s** house.

Words Across the Curriculum

Say each art word. Then, write the word.

1. painters **painters**   3. actors **actors**
2. dancers **dancers**   4. artists **artists**

Write the missing art words.

People enjoy many different kinds of **artists** work. Some people like to visit museums to see their favorite **painters** works of art. Some people enjoy going to a play to see the **actors** performances. Others enjoy watching a group of **dancers** movements onstage.

66

Page 67

Words in Writing

Write a short story about something funny or interesting that happened to you or members of your family. Use at least four words from the box.

Answers will vary.

baby s	friend s	everyone s	families	actors
mother s	sister s	hamster s	grandmothers	dancers
brothers	children s	friends	customers	artists
officer s	family s	father s	painters	

Misspelled Words

Read the story. Circle the four possessive nouns that are used or spelled incorrectly. Then, write the correct possessive nouns.

I was taking care of my best (friends) hamster while he went to his (familys) cabin for a week. On the second morning, the (hamsters) cage was empty. My oldest sister s cat was licking its paws in a corner of my room. I gasped and ran into my parents bedroom. I couldn t understand why they were both laughing. Then, I saw the hamster curled up inside one of my (fathers) slippers.

friend s   **hamster s**

family s   **father s**

67

Page 68

Say each word. Look for familiar and unfamiliar spelling patterns. Then, write the word.

Spelling Tip	Some words have unusual spellings. You have to remember how these words are spelled.

Spelling Words

person	**person**
sure	**sure**
touch	**touch**
tropical	**tropical**
young	**young**
island	**island**
built	**built**
against	**against**
different	**different**
palm	**palm**
awhile	**awhile**
answer	**answer**
mountain	**mountain**
remember	**remember**
camera	**camera**

68

Page 69

Words in Context

Write the missing spelling words.

A Vacation in Paradise Awaits You

Would you like to relax for **awhile** on a quiet beach without having another **person** in sight? If the **answer** to this question is yes, please plan to visit our beautiful **island**. You will be **sure** to enjoy your stay. You can lie in a hammock under a **palm** tree as a cool breeze blows gently **against** your skin. You can wade along the shore and feel the warm **touch** of the sparkling blue ocean.

There are many **different** things to do here, whether you are old or **young**. You can hike up the stone steps that were **built** into the slope of a **mountain** hundreds of years ago. You also can take a walk through our **tropical** rain forest. **Remember** to bring your **camera** so you can take pictures of the beautiful scenery.

69

Answer Key

Answer Key

Page 70

Fun with Words

Alliteration is when a group of words have the same beginning sound. Use alliteration to write the spelling word that best fits each sentence.

1. She s _____ **sure** _____ she saw sheep shivering in the shade.
2. Tourists tried to twist through the trails under the _____ **tropical** _____ trees.
3. Bill _____ **built** _____ a box with black and blue blocks.
4. You ll be _____ **young** _____ for years.
5. The members must _____ **remember** _____ to meet at midnight.
6. Dino demands a _____ **different** _____ dish every day for dinner.
7. Ann acted _____ **against** _____ Aunt Alice s advice.
8. Ken s _____ **camera** _____ captured a captivating shot of the calico cats.
9. We will wait _____ **awhile** _____ for warmer weather.

Words Across the Curriculum

Say each math word. Then, write the word.

1. height _____ **height** _____
2. symbol _____ **symbol** _____
3. cylinder _____ **cylinder** _____
4. graph _____ **graph** _____

Write the math word that completes each sentence.

1. A tube is shaped like a _____ **cylinder** _____ .
2. The volume of a rectangle is its length times its width times its _____ **height** _____ .
3. Ordered pairs can be plotted on a _____ **graph** _____ .
4. The _____ **symbol** _____ for cubic centimeters is cm³.

Page 71

Words in Writing

Write an ad for a vacation spot that you would like to visit. Use at least four words from the box.

Answers will vary.

person	tropical	built	palm	mountain	height	symbol
sure	young	against	awhile	remember	cylinder	graph
touch	island	different	answer	camera		

Dictionary Practice

Use hyphens to show where to divide each word into syllables. Use a dictionary if you need help.

1. camera _____ **cam-er-a** _____
2. mountain _____ **moun-tain** _____
3. answer _____ **an-swer** _____
4. cylinder _____ **cyl-in-der** _____
5. different _____ **dif-fer-ent** _____
6. remember _____ **re-mem-ber** _____
7. measure _____ **mea-sure** _____
8. symbol _____ **sym-bol** _____

Page 72

Say each pair of words. Notice how the spelling of the plural form is different from the singular form. Also notice that one word does not have a singular form. Then, write each plural word.

Spelling Tip	When a noun ends with **f** or **fe**, change the **f** or **fe** to **v** before adding **es**. A few nouns have plural forms that you have to remember.

Spelling Words

leaf	leaves	**leaves**
calf	calves	**calves**
life	lives	**lives**
ox	oxen	**oxen**
wife	wives	**wives**
half	halves	**halves**
mouse	mice	**mice**
wolf	wolves	**wolves**
thief	thieves	**thieves**
loaf	loaves	**loaves**
goose	geese	**geese**
knife	knives	**knives**
shelf	shelves	**shelves**
scarf	scarves	**scarves**
themselves		**themselves**

Page 73

Words in Context

Write the missing spelling words.

Challenge

Circle the other plural nouns in the story.

The Story of Ali Baba

A popular Middle Eastern folktale tells the story of Ali Baba and the forty _____ **thieves** _____ . Ali Baba found the (robbers) secret cave hidden behind the _____ **leaves** _____ of some thick (bushes). Ali Baba listened at the door of the cave. He knew that the (robbers) would attack him like a pack of _____ **wolves** _____ pouncing on a flock of _____ **geese** _____ or a herd of helpless _____ **calves** _____ if they found him there. He heard nothing but a few _____ **mice** _____ nibbling on _____ **loaves** _____ of bread.

When Ali Baba entered the cave, he saw al (kinds) of (treasures) heaped upon _____ **shelves** _____ and (tables). He saw (piles) of gold and valuable (goods), such a (ladies) _____ **scarves** _____ and sharp _____ **knives** _____ with jeweled (handles). Ali Baba loaded a few (bags) of treasure onto his _____ **oxen** _____ .

Ali Baba and his brother Cassim got along well, but their _____ **wives** _____ stirred up trouble. Cassim s wife thought that the (brothers) should split the treasure between _____ **themselves** _____ in two _____ **halves** _____ . Cassim went to the cave and took so much treasure that the (robbers) noticed it was missing. The _____ **lives** _____ of the (brothers) were in danger.

Fun with Words
Write the spelling word that names things you might find in each place.

1. inside a library — **shelves**
2. in a kitchen drawer — **knives**
3. on a branch — **leaves**
4. with cows — **calves**
5. at a pond — **geese**
6. with their husbands — **wives**
7. around people s necks — **scarves**
8. in a bakery — **loaves**
9. in the mountains — **wolves**
10. in prison — **thieves**

Words Across the Curriculum
Say each pair of words. Notice how the spelling of the plural form is different from the singular form. Also notice that one word does not have a singular form. Then, write the plural word.

1. elf elves — **elves**
2. woman women — **women**
3. child children — **children**
4. ourselves — **ourselves**

Write the missing irregular plural nouns.

1. The **children** made sandcastles on the beach.
2. **Elves** are imaginary creatures who sometimes help humans.
3. We are going to the park by **ourselves**.
4. Only a few men and **women** are chosen to be astronauts.

74

Words in Writing
Write your own folktale or fable. Use at least four words from the box.

Answers will vary.

leaves	oxen	mice	loaves	shelves	elves	women
calves	wives	wolves	geese	scarves	children	ourselves
lives	halves	thieves	knives	themselves		

Misspelled Words
Read the fable. Circle the five misspelled words. Then, write the words correctly.

A group of (mouses) once roamed the kitchen of a farmhouse. They climbed up the (shelfs) and tables, eating crumbs from (loafs) of bread and pieces of cheese. When the master of the house bought a cat, they held a meeting among (themselfs) to see how they could outwit the cat.

Let s tie a bell around the cat s neck, said a young mouse.

That s easy to say, replied an older mouse. But who among us will actually risk their (lifes) to become heroes?

mice **loaves** **lives**

shelves **themselves**

75

Say each word. Listen to the final /əl/ sound. Then, write the word.

| Spelling Tip | The /əl/ sound at the ends of words is often spelled **le**. |

Spelling Words

settle	**settle**
angle	**angle**
title	**title**
bubble	**bubble**
trouble	**trouble**
sparkle	**sparkle**
kettle	**kettle**
simple	**simple**
scramble	**scramble**
terrible	**terrible**
puzzle	**puzzle**
scribble	**scribble**
tremble	**tremble**
double	**double**
trickle	**trickle**

76

Words in Context
Write the missing spelling words.

The First (National) Park

| Challenge |
| Circle the other words in the story with the final /əl/ sound spelled **le**. |

Before the 1870s, pioneers had not yet begun to **settle** in Idaho, Wyoming, and Montana. However, explorers told (incredible) stories of hot water that would **bubble** from the ground like water boiling from a **kettle** on a stove. Sometimes, they said the ground seemed to (rumble) and **tremble**. The hot water would spurt straight out of the ground at a right **angle** and **sparkle** in the sunlight. Then, it would slow to a **trickle**. Afraid that something **terrible** might happen to them, the explorers would **scramble** to safety. Still, they took time to **scribble** brief notes about the geysers. How geysers worked was a **puzzle** to early explorers, but it is **simple** to understand.

In 1872, explorers had very (little) **trouble** convincing Congress to set aside this (remarkable) land which became the first (national) park. It contains more than **double** the amount of all the other geysers on Earth. The park s **title** is Yellowstone (National) Park.

77

Answer Key

Fun with Words
Clich s are familiar phrases that have been used over and over again.
Write the spelling word that completes each clich .

I. The truth is pure and ____simple____.

2. This is a fine ____kettle____ of fish!

3. I need to ____settle____ a score with you.

4. Her eyes ____sparkle____ like diamonds.

5. I don t want to burst your ____bubble____, but . . .

6. I started to ____tremble____ like a leaf in the wind.

7. The money began to slowly ____trickle____ in.

8. The detective finally put together the pieces of the ____puzzle____.

Words Across the Curriculum
Say each science word. Then, write the word.

I. ankle ____ankle____   3. cycle ____cycle____

2. muscle ____muscle____   4. particle ____particle____

Write the science word that belongs with each group of words.

I. atom, molecule, ____particle____

2. bone, tendon ____muscle____

3. water, life ____cycle____

4. knee, elbow ____ankle____

78

Words in Writing
Write notes about some things that you know about
water. Use at least four words from the box.

_____

_____

Answers will vary.

_____

_____

settle	bubble	kettle	terrible	tremble	ankle	muscle
angle	trouble	simple	puzzle	double	cycle	particle
title	sparkle	scramble	scribble	trickle		

Misspelled Words
Read the notes about water. Circle the five misspelled words. Then, write
the words correctly.

Water on Earth goes through a simple (sycle).
There s more than (doubele) the amount of water in oceans than in lakes
    and rivers.
(Particels) of water from oceans rise and collect in clouds.
When rain falls to Earth, some water drops (setle) in puddles. Others (trikle)
    from tree branches down to the ground.

____cycle____   ____particles____   ____trickle____

____double____   ____settle____

79

Say each word. Notice the different spellings of the words that sound the
same. Then, write each word.

Spelling Tip	Homophones are words that sound the same but have different spellings and meanings.

Spelling Words

close ____close____

sight ____sight____

poor ____poor____

peek ____peek____

groan ____groan____

waste ____waste____

clothes ____clothes____

miner ____miner____

pour ____pour____

site ____site____

peak ____peak____

waist ____waist____

grown ____grown____

pore ____pore____

minor ____minor____

80

Words in Context
Write the missing spelling words.

San Francisco, 1849

I arrived in San Francisco in 1849 to become a
gold ____miner____. I spent most of my
money to pay my fare on the ship, so now I was
____poor____. I didn t have a penny to ____waste____. This, I
thought, was only a ____minor____ problem. Soon, I d be rich.

With the money I had left, I bought some food and work
____clothes____ at a general store. I put them on and strapped my
belt around my ____waist____. As I paid for my goods, the store
clerk described how the city had ____grown____ in the past year. I
reached behind me to ____close____ the door of the store and
began a new chapter of my life.

I started down the dusty trail with the ____sight____ of a
mountain ____peak____ looming before me. After a few days, I
found a good ____site____ to look for gold. With a loud
____groan____, I dropped my heavy pack. Sweat dripped from every
____pore____ of my skin. As I sat down by the creek bed and began
to ____pour____ water over my head, I saw something sparkling in the
mud. I closed my eyes before I dared to take another ____peek____.

81

Answer Key

Fun with Words

Write the spelling word that completes each quote.

1. It s not the man who has too little that is _____poor_____; it s the man who always wants more. —Unknown

2. Today I have _____grown_____ taller from walking with the trees. —Karl Baker

3. _____Waste_____ not, want not. —Benjamin Franklin

4. A person who is out of _____sight_____ is soon out of mind. —Unknown

5. You can t judge a book by its cover or a man by his _____clothes_____. —Unknown

6. Happiness is a perfume which you cannot _____pour_____ on someone without getting some on yourself. —Ralph Waldo Emerson

Words Across the Curriculum

Say each pair of words that sound the same. The underlined word is the science word. Look at the different spellings. Then, write the science word.

1. scent, sent _____scent_____   3. foul, fowl _____fowl_____

2. beat, beet _____beet_____   4. heel, he ll _____heel_____

Write the science homophone that completes each sentence.

1. A _____beet_____ is a vegetable that grows underground.

2. The rounded, back part of a human foot is the _____heel_____.

3. Ducks and geese are both water _____fowl_____.

4. The color and _____scent_____ of a flower attracts bees.

82

Words in Writing

Make up some wise sayings, or proverbs. Use at least four words from the box.

Answers will vary.

close	peek	clothes	site	grown	scent	beet
sight	groan	miner	peak	pore	fowl	heel
poor	waste	pour	waist	minor		

Dictionary Practice

Read the dictionary entries. Then, write the part of speech and the number of the definition for the underlined word in each sentence.

waste _n._ **1.** The act of using carelessly. **2.** A wild or deserted place with few or no living things. _v._ **1.** To use up or spend in a careless way. **2.** To destroy or ruin.

foul _adj._ **1.** Unpleasant or disgusting. **2.** Very bad; evil. _v._ **1.** To make dirty. **2.** To break a rule in sports, especially by unfairly touching another player.

1. The rotten bananas had a <u>foul</u> smell. _adjective, 1_

2. The invading army <u>wasted</u> everything in its path. _verb, 2_

3. Watching that movie was a <u>waste</u> of time. _noun, 1_

4. I got a free throw because a player on the other team <u>fouled</u> me. _verb, 2_

83

Write the spelling word that is an antonym of each word.

1. same _____different_____

2. rich _____poor_____

3. husbands _____wives_____

4. wonderful _____terrible_____

5. forget _____remember_____

6. old _____young_____

7. complex _____simple_____

8. open _____close_____

9. question _____answer_____

10. for _____against_____

Write the spelling word that belongs with each group of words.

11. eighths, fourths, thirds, _____halves_____

12. chicks, lambs, foals, _____calves_____

13. plates, forks, spoons, _____knives_____

14. hill, volcano, cliff, _____mountain_____

15. point, line, side, _____angle_____

16. riddle, mystery, maze, _____puzzle_____

17. moan, shriek, cry, _____groan_____

18. twice, couple, pair, _____double_____

84

Write the spelling word that is a synonym of each word.

19. made _____built_____

20. robbers _____thieves_____

21. twinkle _____sparkle_____

22. dad s _____father s_____

23. shake _____tremble_____

24. moms _____mothers_____

25. certain _____sure_____

26. name _____title_____

Write the spelling word that completes each sentence.

27. The _____baby s_____ crib was full of toys and blankets.

28. The autumn _____leaves_____ are red and orange.

29. Are there many _____palm_____ trees on this island?

30. Mother likes to bake _____loaves_____ of bread.

31. Do you have your _Answers will vary._ hat on?

32. _____Wolves_____ are members of the dog family.

85

Answer Key

Say each word. Listen for the /j/ sound. Then, write each word.

Spelling Tip	The /j/ sound can be spelled **j, g,** or **dje.**

Spelling Words

bridge	bridge
jazz	jazz
image	image
luggage	luggage
jumble	jumble
range	range
message	message
jockey	jockey
manage	manage
gentle	gentle
plunge	plunge
cabbage	cabbage
lodge	lodge
garbage	garbage
dangerous	dangerous

86

Words in Context
Write the missing spelling words.

> **Challenge**
> Circle the other words in the essay with the /j/ sound.

What to Do?

Grown-ups always ask what I want to do when I grow up. There s such a (large) ____range____ of things to do that I haven t decided yet. I d like to be a ____jockey____, but that would be very ____dangerous____. Racehorses aren t known for being ____gentle____ animals. I m afraid I d fall off and ____plunge____ to the ground with my arms and legs all in a ____jumble____. I can (just) (imagine) the X-ray ____image____ of all the (damaged) bones in my body.

I wouldn t mind working in a ski ____lodge____. I could help the skiers take their ____luggage____ to their rooms and give them a ____message____ when someone wants to reach them. Or, I could work in the kitchen, chopping up ____cabbage____ and other (vegetables.) I d probably have to clean the whole kitchen and take out the ____garbage____, too. On second thought, if I worked in a ski resort, I d want to ____manage____ all the other workers. Or, I could be an (engineer) and design the longest ____bridge____ in the world. I could play in a ____jazz____ band at night.

87

Fun with Words
Write the spelling word that answers each clue.

1. If you travel a lot, you have to lug me around. ____luggage____

2. I come from ragtime and the blues. Bebop, rock, and hip-hop came from me. ____jazz____

3. My job is racing, but I don t run. ____jockey____

4. You see me when you look in a mirror. ____image____

5. Nobody likes me; everyone always wants to get rid of me. ____garbage____

6. I bring places together. ____bridge____

7. I am the head of the garden. ____cabbage____

8. I shelter people in the woods and mountains. ____lodge____

Words Across the Curriculum
Say each social studies word. Then, write the word.

1. jury ____jury____   3. badge ____badge____
2. gypsy ____gypsy____   4. justice ____justice____

Write the social studies word that completes each sentence.

1. A police officer wears a ____badge____ to identify himself or herself.

2. The court system is meant to provide ____justice____ for all citizens.

3. We heard singing and clapping coming from the ____gypsy____ camp.

4. A judge or a ____jury____ can make a decision in a legal trial.

88

Words in Writing
Describe a trip that you d like to take. Use at least four words from the box.

Answers will vary.

bridge	luggage	message	gentle	dangerous	jury	gypsy
jazz	jumble	jockey	plunge	lodge	badge	justice
image	range	manage	cabbage	garbage		

Misspelled Words
Read the description. Circle the four misspelled words. Then, write the words correctly.

I d like to stay at a ski (lodje) in the mountains. As soon as I got there, I d take my (luggadge) to my room and put on my ski clothes. I d leave a (messaje) for my parents that I would be on the slopes all day. I d get my ski badge, ride the ski lift up a mountain, and (plundge) down the slope.

____lodge____   ____message____

____luggage____   ____plunge____

89

Answer Key

Say each word. Listen for the /k/ sound. Then, write each word.

Spelling Tip	The /k/ sound can be spelled **c**, **k**, and **ck**.

Spelling Words

junk	junk
socket	socket
carpet	carpet
kangaroo	kangaroo
corner	corner
picnic	picnic
ticket	ticket
candle	candle
bucket	bucket
creaky	creaky
attack	attack
plastic	plastic
racket	racket
attic	attic
hockey	hockey

90

Words in Context
Write the missing spelling words.

Be Careful of Rainy Days

Challenge
Circle the other words in the story with the /k/ sound.

One rainy day last week, I decided to explore the __attic__. Holding out a lit __candle__ in front of me, I crept up the __creaky__ old stairs. They were barely covered by a worn-out __carpet__. I kept looking back over my shoulder as if someone might sneak up and __attack__ me from behind.

When I got to the top of the stairs, I looked around and saw all kinds of __junk__. In one __corner__, there was a rusty metal __bucket__ next to a wicker __picnic__ basket. Next to these was a trunk filled with sports equipment including a __hockey__ stick, ice skates, and a tennis __racket__. Nearby, a stuffed __kangaroo__ seemed to stare at me with one __plastic__ black eye. Scattered across an old desk were letters, postcards, and even an old movie __ticket__.

Suddenly, I heard footsteps behind me on the stairs. My mother appeared and plugged a lamp into a __socket__. I'm so glad you're here to help me clean up this mess, she said with a wicked smile.

91

Fun with Words
Write the spelling word that fits each comparison.

1. *Curtain* is to *window* as __carpet__ is to *floor*.
2. *Soccer* is to *grass* as __hockey__ is to *ice*.
3. *Basement* is to *bottom* as __attic__ is to *top*.
4. *Snake* is to *slither* as __kangaroo__ is to *hop*.
5. *Bat* is to *baseball* as __racket__ is to *tennis*.
6. *Straw* is to *basket* as *metal* is to __bucket__.
7. *Bulb* is to *flashlight* as *flame* is to __candle__.
8. *Curve* is to *circle* as __corner__ is to *square*.
9. *Hug* is to *friend* as __attack__ is to *enemy*.
10. *Lunchbox* is to *lunch* as *basket* is to __picnic__.

Words Across the Curriculum
Say each science word. Then, write the word.

1. climate __climate__
2. cricket __cricket__
3. volcano __volcano__
4. compound __compound__

Write each science word next to its definition.

1. a substance made of two or more elements __compound__
2. a hopping insect related to a grasshopper __cricket__
3. a mountain that ejects lava and hot rocks __volcano__
4. the weather patterns in an area __climate__

92

Words in Writing
Describe a place in your home where many things are stored. Use at least four words from the box.

Answers will vary.

junk	kangaroo	ticket	creaky	racket	climate	volcano
socket	corner	candle	attack	attic	compound	cricket
carpet	picnic	bucket	plastic	hockey		

Dictionary Practice
Write four words from the box that have each sound listed below. You might use a word in more than one column.

Short a Sound	Short i Sound	Short o Sound
attic	attic	hockey
attack	ticket	socket
racket	cricket	compound
candle	picnic	volcano

93

Answer Key

Page 94

Say each word. Listen for the /s/ sound. Then, write each word.

Spelling Tip	The /s/ sound can be spelled **c** or **s**.

Spelling Words

silent	silent
suit	suit
special	special
sorry	sorry
notice	notice
ceiling	ceiling
promise	promise
sudden	sudden
cereal	cereal
select	select
circus	circus
office	office
sentence	sentence
balance	balance
celebrate	celebrate

94

Page 95

Words in Context
Write the missing spelling words.

Challenge
Circle the other words in the story with the /s/ sound.

Birthday Surprise

Last Saturday was my birthday. As I was eating my breakfast of **cereal** and juice, my dad came downstairs. He was dressed in a **suit** and tie. He looked like he was ready to go to his **office** and work. He had forgotten his **promise** to spend his **special** day with me.

My dad was very **sorry** that he had forgotten. He took me to the mall and let me **select** some games and CDs. Then, we went to the **circus**. We had a great time there. I especially enjoyed watching the acrobats **balance** on the high wire.

When we got back home, our house was dark and **silent**. I didn't **notice** anything unusual. All of a **sudden**, the lights went on. The **ceiling** was covered with floating balloons and a banner with a **sentence** that said, Have a great year! My friends were all there to **celebrate** my birthday!

95

Page 96

Fun with Words
Solve the puzzle with spelling words.

Across
2. a set of clothes
4. words that express a complete thought
6. a vow or word of honor
7. breakfast food
8. fast and without warning

Down
1. see
3. a place to do paperwork
4. without sound
5. a traveling show

Crossword answers:
2. suit
4. sentence
6. promise
7. cereal
8. sudden
1. notice
3. office
4. silent
5. circus

Words Across the Curriculum
Say each science word. Then, write the word.

1. solid — solid
2. surface — surface
3. icicle — icicle
4. science — science

Write each science word next to the pair of words it belongs with.

1. outside, top — surface
2. frost, snow — icicle
3. math, art — science
4. gas, liquid — solid

96

Page 97

Words in Writing
Write about a day that was important to you. Use at least four words from the box.

Answers will vary.

silent	sorry	promise	select	sentence	solid	surface
suit	notice	sudden	circus	balance	icicle	science
special	ceiling	cereal	office	celebrate		

Misspelled Words
Read the description. Circle the five misspelled words. Then, write the words correctly.

Last winter, there was a suddin snowstorm during the night. When I went outside the next morning, I noticed that everything was cilent and covered with snow. The surfase of our pond was frozen solud. My sister and I skated on the pond all day. I was sory when the day ended.

sudden	surface	sorry
silent	solid	

97

Answer Key

Say each word. Look for familiar spelling patterns. Then, write each word.

Spelling Tip	The **ex-** spelling usually comes at the beginnings of words.

Spelling Words

except	except
example	example
exciting	exciting
exactly	exactly
extend	extend
expect	expect
excuse	excuse
explain	explain
express	express
exert	exert
exercise	exercise
exhausted	exhausted
excellent	excellent
expensive	expensive
extremely	extremely

98

Words in Context
Write the missing spelling words.

Challenge
Circle the other words in the essay with **ex**.

Why Not Try Tennis?

Playing tennis is an __excellent__ way to __exercise__ while playing a fun sport. The match I recently played is a perfect __example__. I didn t really __expect__ the match to __extend__ any longer than an hour. However, the match ended up taking __exactly__ two hours and twenty-two minutes. I had to __exert__ every (extra) bit of energy I had to finish the match, but I still lost. I tried not to __express__ my disappointment about losing. Afterwards, my opponent and I were both __exhausted__. We were moving __extremely__ slowly when we (exited) the tennis court.

Some people tell me that they don t play tennis because it s too __expensive__. I think that they just say this as an __excuse__ not to play. I __explain__ to them that once they have a racket and tennis shoes, they don t have to spend any more money __except__ to buy new tennis balls once in a while. I also tell them that you don t have to be an (expert) player to enjoy tennis. It s an __exciting__ game that everyone should try.

99

Fun with Words
Write the spelling word that fits each sentence and rhymes with the underlined word.

1. The police __expect__ to question the <u>suspect</u>.
2. Isn t it __exciting__ that they re <u>inviting</u> us to the concert?
3. I d like to __express__ my joy for your <u>success</u>.
4. Please __explain__ why you continue to <u>complain</u>.
5. That <u>sample</u> is an __example__ of sandy soil.
6. My mom didn t <u>refuse</u> to __excuse__ me from school today.
7. This spray seems to be an __excellent__ insect <u>repellant</u>.
8. I had to __exert__ my strongest effort to stay awake and <u>alert</u>.

Words Across the Curriculum
Say each science word. Then, write the word.

1. examine __examine__   3. exhibit __exhibit__
2. explode __explode__   4. experiment __experiment__

Write the science word or words that complete each sentence.

1. A dinosaur __exhibit__ is on display at the museum.
2. It s important to __examine__ the results of an __experiment__ before drawing a conclusion.
3. Some chemicals __explode__ when they come in contact with oxygen.

100

Words in Writing
Write a persuasive paragraph about a sport you enjoy. Use at least four words from the box.

_____

_____

Answers will vary.

except	exactly	excuse	exert	excellent	examine	explode
example	extend	explain	exercise	expensive	exhibit	experiment
exciting	expect	express	exhausted	extremely		

Dictionary Practice
Write the words from the box in alphabetical order. You will have to look at the third or fourth letter of each word.

1. __exactly__   8. __exercise__   15. __explain__
2. __examine__   9. __exert__   16. __explode__
3. __example__   10. __exhausted__ 17. __express__
4. __excellent__   11. __exhibit__   18. __extend__
5. __except__   12. __expect__   19. __extremely__
6. __exciting__   13. __expensive__
7. __excuse__   14. __experiment__

101

Spectrum Spelling
Grade 4

Answer Key

Write the spelling word that rhymes with each word.

1. confess   express
2. mumble   jumble
3. picket   ticket
4. boot   suit
5. refuse   excuse
6. peeling   ceiling
7. squeaky   creaky
8. complain   explain
9. handle   candle
10. has   jazz
11. sponge   plunge
12. jacket   racket
13. inviting   exciting
14. bunk   junk
15. pocket   socket

102

Write the spelling word that belongs with each pair of words.

16. baseball, soccer,   hockey
17. word, paragraph,   sentence
18. model, sample,   example
19. cabin, inn,   lodge
20. rug, mat,   carpet
21. basement, garage,   attic
22. letter, note,   message

Write the spelling word that is a synonym of each word.

23. pail   bucket
24. trash   garbage
25. very   extremely
26. unsafe   dangerous
27. quiet   silent
28. choose   select
29. tired   exhausted
30. operate   manage
31. costly   expensive

103

Say each word. Listen to the first syllable. Then, write each word.

Spelling Tip	The prefix **in-** can mean *not* or *in*. The prefix **re-** often means *again*. The prefix **un-** means *not*.

Spelling Words

remove	remove
unfair	unfair
instant	instant
regret	regret
unable	unable
instead	instead
review	review
unaware	unaware
invent	invent
repeat	repeat
unless	unless
incorrect	incorrect
retreat	retreat
refuse	refuse
incomplete	incomplete

104

Words in Context
Write the missing spelling words.

Going Fishing

	Challenge
	Circle the other words in the journal entry with the suffixes **in-**, **re-**, and **un-**.

On Saturday morning, my mom made me ____review____ my latest math exam. I had seven ____incorrect____ answers, and one problem was ____incomplete____ because I hadn t had time to finish it. I had to ____repeat____ all of my calculations. The ____instant____ I finished, my best friend called and (invited) me to go fishing with him.

I was ____unaware____ that my dad had other plans for me. He told me to clean my room ____instead____ of going fishing. I thought it was ____unfair____ of him to (interrupt) my plans, but I couldn t ____refuse____ to clean my room. I was ____unable____ to ____invent____ any excuses, but I did ____regret____ all those times when I left my clothes lying on the floor.

I was forced to ____retreat____ into my messy bedroom. ____Unless____ I could clean it up quickly, I would have to forget about fishing. For the next half-hour, I worked (incredibly) hard to ____remove____ every piece of trash and dirty clothing from my room. Finally, I was free to go fishing.

105

Answer Key

Words in Writing

Write a paragraph about something you cannot do very well. Use at least four words from the box.

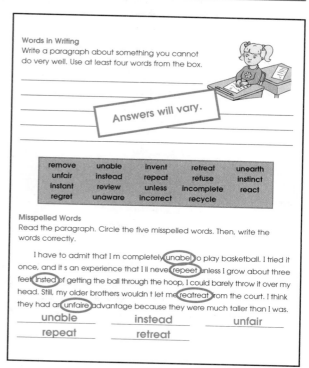

Answers will vary.

remove	unable	invent	retreat	unearth
unfair	instead	repeat	refuse	instinct
instant	review	unless	incomplete	react
regret	unaware	incorrect	recycle	

Misspelled Words

Read the paragraph. Circle the five misspelled words. Then, write the words correctly.

I have to admit that I'm completely (unabel) to play basketball. I tried it once, and it's an experience that I'll never (repeet) unless I grow about three feet. (Insted) of getting the ball through the hoop, I could barely throw it over my head. Still, my older brothers wouldn't let me (reatreat) from the court. I think they had an (unfaire) advantage because they were much taller than I was.

unable **instead** **unfair**

repeat **retreat**

107

Say each word. Listen to the first syllable. Then, write each word.

| **Spelling Tip** | The prefix **dis-** often means *the opposite of.* The prefix **mis-** often means *wrong or a lack of.* |

Spelling Words

dislike	**dislike**
mistake	**mistake**
disturb	**disturb**
dismiss	**dismiss**
misery	**misery**
dishonest	**dishonest**
disease	**disease**
misplaced	**misplaced**
discuss	**discuss**
disappoint	**disappoint**
disagree	**disagree**
misfortune	**misfortune**
discover	**discover**
disappear	**disappear**
distribute	**distribute**

108

Words in Context

Write the missing spelling words.

Challenge

Circle the other words in the story with the /k/ sound.

Be (Careful) of Rainy Days

One rainy day last (week,) I decided to explore the **attic**. Holding out a lit **candle** in front of me, I (crept) up the **creaky** old stairs. They were barely (covered) by a worn-out **carpet**. I (kept) (looking) (back) over my shoulder as if someone might (sneak) up and **attack** me from behind.

When I got to the top of the stairs, I looked around and saw all (kinds) of **junk**. In one **corner**, there was a rusty metal **bucket** next to a (wicker) **picnic** (basket.) Next to these was a (trunk) filled with sports equipment (including) a **hockey** (stick,) (ice) (skates,) and a tennis **racket**. Nearby, a stuffed **kangaroo** seemed to stare at me with one **plastic** (black) eye. (Scattered) (across) an old (desk) were letters, (postcards,) and even an old movie **ticket**.

Suddenly, I heard footsteps behind me on the stairs. My mother appeared and plugged a lamp into a **socket**. I'm so glad you're here to help me (clean) up this mess, she said with a (wicked) smile.

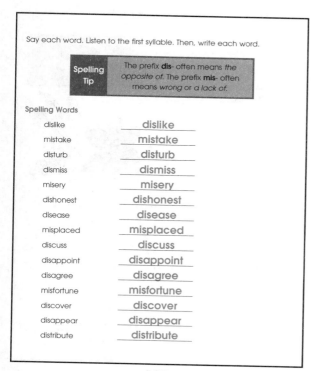

109

Spectrum Spelling
Grade 4

Answer Key

Fun with Words

Write the spelling word that belongs to the same word family as each word below.

1. placement   misplaced
2. likely   dislike
3. agreement   disagree
4. easily   disease
5. fortunately   misfortune
6. appointment   disappoint
7. mission   dismiss
8. covering   discover

Words Across the Curriculum

Say each language arts word. Then, write the word.

1. misprint   misprint
2. misquote   misquote
3. misspelled   misspelled
4. display   display

Write the missing language arts words.

A newspaper editor has to make sure that a reporter doesn t _____misquote_____ a person who gives information. The editor edits articles to correct any _____misspelled_____ words and tries to avoid any kind of _____misprint_____ in the paper. The editor also chooses photos to _____display_____ with the articles.

110

Words in Writing

Write directions that tell how you would research and write a newspaper article. Use at least four words from the box.

Answers will vary.

dislike	misery	discuss	discover	misspelled
mistake	dishonest	disappoint	disappear	misquote
disturb	disease	disagree	distribute	display
dismiss	misplaced	misfortune	misprint	

Dictionary Practice

Write *noun*, *verb*, or *adjective* to tell what part of speech each word is.

1. discover   verb
2. misery   noun
3. dishonest   adjective
4. disease   noun
5. disturb   verb
6. misfortune   noun
7. disagree   verb
8. disappear   verb

111

Say each word. Listen to the last syllable. Then, write each word.

Spelling Tip	Many adverbs end with **ly**.

Spelling Words

lonely	lonely
wisely	wisely
barely	barely
rapidly	rapidly
finally	finally
truly	truly
secretly	secretly
closely	closely
eagerly	eagerly
safely	safely
totally	totally
freely	freely
perfectly	perfectly
certainly	certainly
personally	personally

112

Words in Context

Write the missing spelling words.

Born Free

Challenge
Circle the other words in the story that end with the suffix — **ly**.

My dad was resting in his hammock so comfortably that he was _____barely_____ awake. A _____truly_____ beautiful butterfly with _____perfectly_____ matched markings on its wings fluttered by him so _____rapidly_____ that hardly saw it. My dad suddenly became alert and _____closely_____ watched the butterfly as it landed on a nearby flower. I _____personally_____ don t know anything about butterflies, but my dad does. He _____eagerly_____ crept towards it with a net, and I _____wisely_____ remained _____totally_____ silent. _____Secretly_____, I hoped that my dad wouldn t catch the butterfly. I thought it belonged in the garden, moving _____freely_____ from flower to flower. If my dad kept it inside a terrarium, it would _____certainly_____ be very _____lonely_____ all by itself. _____Finally_____, my dad had his net just above the butterfly when our dog suddenly an over to him and began barking loudly Just in time, the butterfly flew _____safely_____ away from the net.

113

Spectrum Spelling
Grade 4

186

Answer Key

Answer Key

Page 114

Fun with Words

Unscramble the underlined words to make spelling words. If there is more than one word underlined, combine both words, then unscramble them.

1. A <u>gray eel</u> slithered through the water. — eagerly
2. The <u>tall</u> boy got a new <u>toy</u> for his birthday. — totally
3. Did you see the gull <u>fly</u> over the <u>sea</u>? — safely
4. The children began to <u>cry</u> when they saw the <u>sleet</u> outside. — secretly
5. We worked <u>nicely</u> together on our <u>art</u> projects. — certainly
6. That <u>lady</u> has a <u>rip</u> in her coat. — rapidly
7. The soup is made of beef and <u>barley</u>. — barely
8. The farmer <u>nearly</u> slipped when he fed the <u>slop</u> to the pigs. — personally

Words Across the Curriculum

Say each social studies word. Then, write the word.

1. recently — recently
2. monthly — monthly
3. daily — daily
4. weekly — weekly

Write each social studies word next to its meaning.

1. every day — daily
2. not long ago — recently
3. once every seven days — weekly
4. once every 28 to 31 days — monthly

Page 115

Words in Writing

Write a newspaper article that describes a weather event. Use at least four words from the box.

Answers will vary.

lonely	rapidly	secretly	safely	perfectly	recently	monthly
wisely	finally	closely	totally	certainly	daily	weekly
barely	truly	eagerly	freely	personally		

Misspelled Words

Read the article. Circle the five misspelled words. Then, write the words correctly.

A sudden storm swept (rapidly) though the city today. Some people (egerly) reported that they (bearly) got safely inside their houses before the storm hit. Others said that they (personaly) saw a funnel cloud developing. They (wisly) took shelter in the basements of their homes.

rapidly   barely   wisely
eagerly   personally

Page 116

Say each word. Listen to the last syllable. Then, write each word.

| Spelling Tip | The suffix **-ful** means *full of.* The suffix **-less** means *without.* |

Spelling Words

cheerful	cheerful
colorful	colorful
spotless	spotless
thankful	thankful
graceful	graceful
harmless	harmless
hopeful	hopeful
restless	restless
wonderful	wonderful
frightful	frightful
breathless	breathless
thoughtful	thoughtful
faithful	faithful
motionless	motionless
beautiful	beautiful

Page 117

Words in Context

Write the missing spelling words.

Challenge

Circle the other words with the suffix **-ful** or **-less.**

Thanks for the Memories

Dear Ms. Johnson,

I m very ___thankful___ to you for the ___wonderful___ time I had at your camp. I didn t see any ___frightful___ spiders; the cabin was so clean that it was truly ___spotless___. The ___colorful___ blend of blues and yellows inside the cabin always made me feel ___cheerful___. Also, the view of the (peaceful) meadow was ___beautiful___.

Whenever I got ___restless___ from being inside the cabin, I found many things to do outside. I enjoyed observing the ___graceful___ deer running through the woods. Although I was ___breathless___ with excitement to be so close to them, I was (careful) to remain ___motionless___ so they would know that I was ___harmless___.

I also want to let you know how (grateful) I am to your camp workers for being so (helpful) and ___thoughtful___. I am ___hopeful___ that I will be able to return to your camp next year. I will always be a ___faithful___ customer.

Sincerely,
Frankie Martinez

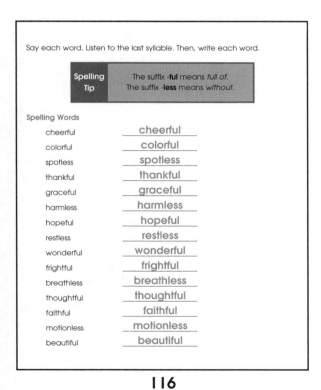

Answer Key

Fun with Words
Write the spelling word that fits each description.

1. A runner after a race — breathless
2. A rainbow in the sky — colorful
3. A scary costume — frightful
4. A person making a wish — hopeful
5. A room that s just been cleaned — spotless
6. A bike that no one is riding — motionless
7. A happy person — cheerful
8. A bee that doesn t sting — harmless
9. A dog that loves its owner — faithful
10. A student writing a report — thoughtful

Words Across the Curriculum
Say each social studies word. Then, write the word.

1. careless — careless
2. eventful — eventful
3. worthless — worthless
4. respectful — respectful

Write the social studies word next to its meaning.

1. without value — worthless
2. full of courtesy — respectful
3. full of things to see and do — eventful
4. without caution or attention — careless

118

Words in Writing
Write a letter thanking someone for something they did for you. Use at least four words from the box.

Answers will vary.

cheerful	graceful	wonderful	faithful	worthless
colorful	harmless	frightful	motionless	eventful
spotless	hopeful	breathless	beautiful	respectful
thankful	restless	thoughtful	careless	

Dictionary Practice
Write the root word of each spelling word below.

1. colorful — color
2. graceful — grace
3. breathless — breath
4. thoughtful — thought
5. wonderful — wonder
6. harmless — harm
7. thankful — thank
8. beautiful — beauty

119

Write the spelling word that is an antonym of each word.

1. ungrateful — thankful
2. dangerous — harmless
3. happiness — misery
4. truthful — dishonest
5. slowly — rapidly
6. openly — secretly
7. ugly — beautiful
8. clumsy — graceful
9. foolishly — wisely
10. alert — unaware

Write the spelling word that completes each sentence.

11. I can t leave __unless__ I ask my dad.
12. My brother looks __frightful__ in his skeleton costume.
13. The frog hopped away the __instant__ I let go of it.
14. Sydney __misplaced__ her book and searched the whole house for it.
15. We have to __remove__ our muddy shoes before we go inside.

120

Write the spelling word that is a synonym of each word.

16. wrong — incorrect
17. illness — disease
18. surely — certainly
19. completely — totally
20. loyal — faithful
21. create — invent
22. unmoving — motionless
23. find — discover
24. error — mistake
25. unluckiness — misfortune
26. honestly — truly
27. happy — cheerful
28. redo — repeat
29. lastly — finally
30. bother — disturb

121

Answer Key

Say each word. Look for familiar spelling patterns. Then, write each word.

Spelling Tip	Many number words have familiar spelling patterns.

Spelling Words

thirty	thirty
sixteen	sixteen
eleven	eleven
billion	billion
forty	forty
thirteen	thirteen
fifteen	fifteen
eighteen	eighteen
fifty	fifty
fourteen	fourteen
million	million
nineteen	nineteen
twenty	twenty
seventeen	seventeen
twelve	twelve

122

Words in Writing
Write the missing spelling words.

Challenge
Circle the other words that name numbers or specific amounts.

Numbers

Numbers can be added and described in all kinds of ways. For example, __twelve__ eggs or doughnuts make a dozen. Two quarters equal __fifty__ cents. three dimes equal __thirty__ cents, and three nickels equal __fifteen__ cents. Two weeks include __fourteen__ days, and two baseball teams have __eighteen__ players on the field at one time.

Two spiders together have __sixteen__ legs. Ten squares have __forty__ angles, while three triangles plus two squares have __seventeen__ angles. One less than a dozen is __eleven__, and one more is __thirteen__. Two times ten is __twenty__, and one less than that is __nineteen__.

Very large numbers describe some other things. Coal and oil formed more than a __million__ years ago. There are more than a __billion__ stars in our galaxy.

123

Fun with Words
Solve each math problem with a numeral that represents a spelling word. Then, write the spelling word.

1. 10 + 7 = __17__ seventeen
2. 100 — 50 = __50__ fifty
3. 32 2 = __16__ sixteen
4. 6 x 5 = __30__ thirty
5. 77 7 = __11__ eleven
6. 5 x 8 = __40__ forty
7. 40 —28 = __12__ twelve
8. 90 6 = __15__ fifteen
9. 39 3 = __13__ thirteen
10. 10 x 2 = __20__ twenty

Words Across the Curriculum
Say each math word. Then, write the word.

1. numeral __numeral__   3. decimal __decimal__
2. product __product__   4. fraction __fraction__

Write the word or words that complete each sentence.

1. A __fraction__ is a part of a whole that can also be represented as a __decimal__.
2. Any number can be spelled out or written as a __numeral__.
3. A __product__ results from multiplying two or more numbers.

124

Words in Writing
Write a paragraph describing what you might be doing at different ages in your life. Use at least four words from the box.

__Answers will vary.__

thirty	billion	fifteen	fourteen	twenty	numeral	product
sixteen	forty	eighteen	million	seventeen	decimal	fraction
eleven	thirteen	fifty	nineteen	twelve		

Misspelled Words
Read the paragraph. Circle the five misspelled words. Then, write the words correctly.

Right now, I m elevin years old. When I turn forteen, I ll be a teenager. I will be glad to get my diver s license when I m sixteen. When I m eigtfteen, I ll be able to vote. Maybe I ll make a millon dollars by the time I m thirtey.

eleven	eighteen	thirty
fourteen	million	

125

Answer Key

Say each word. Listen to the last syllable. Then, write each word.

Spelling Tip	The /shen/ sound is often spelled **tion**. The /cher/ sound is often spelled **ture**. The /yer/ sound is often spelled **ure**.

Spelling Words

nation	nation
moisture	moisture
direction	direction
figure	figure
mention	mention
creature	creature
vacation	vacation
pleasure	pleasure
condition	condition
location	location
feature	feature
attention	attention
adventure	adventure
protection	protection
furniture	furniture

126

Words in Context
Write the missing spelling words.

Challenge
Circle the other words in the ad with **tion**, **ture**, and **ure**.

Dream House

Are you looking for the perfect __vacation__ home for you and your family? We have a house for sale in a wonderful __location__ on the beach. The house is the (creation) of a famous builder. It s in excellent __condition__, and some of the __furniture__ and (pictures) inside will be sold with the house. There s a huge deck that faces in the __direction__ of the ocean. It s a real __pleasure__ to sit so close to the shore that you can feel the __moisture__ from the waves on your skin.

Another great __feature__ of the house is that it s next to one of the most secluded (nature) preserves in the __nation__. You re (sure) to have an interesting __adventure__ every time you visit it. It s common for an unusual __figure__ moving in the preserve to catch the __attention__ of a person walking near it. The (motion) is often caused by an unusual __creature__ that is under the __protection__ of the government.

Please call us and __mention__ this ad. Hurry! This (treasure) will be gone in the very near (future.)

127

Fun with Words
Write the two spelling words that fit each sentence and have the same ending as the underlined word.

1. Please turn your __attention__ to the __direction__ of the motion picture on the screen.
2. It s always a great to have an __adventure__ surrounded by nature.
3. Did you mention the __location__ of your favorite place to take a __vacation__?
4. I hope there won t be any __moisture__ on the patio __furniture__ in the future.
5. The shadowy form of a mysterious __creature__ appeared in the pasture.

Words Across the Curriculum
Say each science word. Then, write the word.

1. caution __caution__   3. solution __solution__
2. measure __measure__   4. temperature __temperature__

Write the science word or words that complete each sentence.

1. Ocean water is a common __solution__ made of salt and water.
2. You can __measure__ the __temperature__ of an object in degrees Fahrenheit or Celsius.
3. Always use __caution__ when working with chemicals.

128

Words in Writing
Write an ad that you could use to convince people to buy something that you own. Use at least four words from the box.

_____

_____

Answers will vary.

_____

_____

_____

nation	mention	condition	adventure	solution
moisture	creature	location	protection	measure
direction	vacation	feature	furniture	temperature
figure	pleasure	attention	caution	

Dictionary Practice
Write the root word of each word below. Use a dictionary if you need help.

1. location __locate__   5. protection __protect__
2. moisture __moist__   6. vacation __vacate__
3. direction __direct__   7. attention __attend__
4. pleasure __please__   8. adventure __venture__

129

Answer Key

Say each word. Listen to the second syllable and the third syllable, if there is one. Then, write each word.

Spelling Tip	For adjectives that end with **y**, change the **y** to **i** before adding **er** or **est**.

Spelling Words

happy	happy
cloudy	cloudy
uglier	uglier
heaviest	heaviest
pretty	pretty
happier	happier
cloudiest	cloudiest
ugly	ugly
heavier	heavier
happiest	happiest
prettier	prettier
ugliest	ugliest
heavy	heavy
cloudier	cloudier
prettiest	prettiest

130

Words in Context

Write the missing spelling words.

An Unkind Princess

There once was a princess who was never _____happier_____ than when she was playing with her golden balls. One _____cloudy_____ day, the princess took three balls that she thought were _____prettier_____ than the others into the garden. Although they were _____heavy_____, the princess liked to toss them into the air. The princess thought they were the _____prettiest_____ sight she had ever seen. As she played, the _____heaviest_____ of the balls rolled into a deep well. The princess was not _____happy_____ about this, and she began to cry. Soon, an _____ugly_____ frog poked his head out of the water.

I ll get the ball if I can eat lunch with you at your dining table, said the frog. Then, I ll be the _____happiest_____ creature in the world instead of the _____ugliest_____.

The princess s face became _____cloudier_____ than the sky as she imagined the frog at her father s fine table. The frog seemed _____uglier_____ to her than ever. Still, the sky was the _____cloudiest_____ that she had ever seen. The princess couldn t go inside without her _____pretty_____ golden ball. Her heart felt _____heavier_____ every minute.

131

Fun with Words

Unscramble the underlined words to make spelling words. If there is more than one word underlined, combine both words, then unscramble them.

1. As I began to eat my <u>rice</u>, I heard a <u>loud</u> noise. _____cloudier_____

2. Be careful not to <u>trip</u> on the rocks under the <u>tree</u>. _____prettier_____

3. Let s <u>eat</u> the honey from the bee s <u>hives</u>. _____heaviest_____

4. I made a small <u>ship</u> out of paper and <u>tape</u>. _____happiest_____

5. When my <u>pet</u> mouse gets tired, <u>it</u> likes to <u>rest</u> on my lap. _____prettiest_____

6. Mother took the pie <u>out</u> of the oven and <u>sliced</u> it into pieces. _____cloudiest_____

Words Across the Curriculum

Say each science word. Then, write the word.

1. sunnier _____sunnier_____   3. healthier _____healthier_____
2. sunniest _____sunniest_____   4. healthiest _____healthiest_____

Write the missing science words.

The _____healthiest_____ plants get just the right amount of sunlight and water. Some plants need to be grown in _____sunnier_____ locations than other plants. A plant that needs constant light might need to be moved to the _____sunniest_____ spot you can find. The plant will soon become _____healthier_____.

132

Words in Writing

Write an ending to the story about the princess and the frog. Use at least four words from the box.

Answers will vary.

happy	heaviest	cloudiest	happiest	heavy	sunnier	sunniest
cloudy	pretty	ugly	prettier	cloudier	healthier	healthiest
uglier	happier	heavier	ugliest	prettiest		

Misspelled Words

Read the ending to the story. Circle the four misspelled words. Then, write the words correctly.

The king was not (happi) with his daughter for trying to break her promise to the frog. He told her that her actions were much (ugleir) than the way the poor frog looked to her. He ordered the princess to find the frog as soon as the cloudy sky became (sunnyier.) The princess was sorry that she had been so cruel to the frog. When she found him, she felt much (happyier.)

_____happy_____   _____sunnier_____

_____uglier_____   _____happier_____

133

Answer Key

Say each word. Look for familiar and unfamiliar spelling patterns. Then, write the word.

Spelling Tip	Some words have unusual spellings. You have to remember how these words are spelled.

Spelling Words

believe	believe
guess	guess
century	century
machine	machine
library	library
probably	probably
recognize	recognize
separate	separate
question	question
portrait	portrait
citizen	citizen
enough	enough
government	government
biography	biography
especially	especially

134

Words in Context
Write the missing spelling words.

Time for Research

For social studies class, I had to read a **biography** about a person whose work I **believe** was **especially** important to my daily life. I didn t have **enough** information at home, so I went to the **library** to do some research. I wanted a quiet place to work, so I found a desk that was **separate** from the main research area.

I wasn t sure whether I wanted to read about a person who invented an important **machine** or a person who helped form the **government** of our country. I was gazing around the room when I saw a **portrait** of a person I didn t **recognize**. My **guess** was that it was **probably** a famous **citizen** from the eighteenth **century**. My **question** was soon answered. The plaque under the painting identified the person as the founder of the city.

135

Fun with Words
Write the spelling word that completes each analogy.

1. Command is to order as **question** is to ask.
2. Member is to club as **citizen** is to country.
3. Theater is to movie as **library** is to book.
4. Statue is to sculpture as **portrait** is to painting.
5. Combine is to unite as **separate** is to divide.
6. Hammer is to tool as car is to **machine**.
7. Fact is to know as faith is to **believe**.
8. Ten is to decade as one hundred is to **century**.
9. Surely is to certainly as possibly is to **probably**.

Words Across the Curriculum
Say each science word. Then, write the word.

1. weather **weather**
2. equator **equator**
3. dinosaur **dinosaur**
4. stomach **stomach**

Write the missing science words.

1. The **equator** separates the northern and southern hemispheres.
2. A **dinosaur** skeleton contains hundreds of bones.
3. Different climates on Earth experience different types of **weather**.
4. A female kangaroo has a pouch on her **stomach** for carrying babies.

136

Words in Writing
Write a paragraph about an important American citizen. Use at least four words from the box.

Answers will vary.

believe	machine	recognize	portrait	biography	weather	equator
guess	library	separate	citizen	especially	dinosaur	stomach
century	probably	question	enough	government		

Dictionary Practice
Write the spelling words that fit in each column below. Some words belong in more than one column.

/e/ Sound	Long e Sound	Long i Sound
guess	believe	recognize
especially	machine	biography
recognize	especially	library
question	library	dinosaur
century	probably	
weather	biography	
	enough	
	equator	

137

Answer Key

Say each word. Look for the two smaller words in each compound word. Then, write the word.

Spelling Tip	Many compound words are made of smaller words with familiar spelling patterns.

Spelling Words

highway	highway
football	football
classmate	classmate
skateboard	skateboard
motorcycle	motorcycle
newspaper	newspaper
background	background
notebook	notebook
stoplight	stoplight
sideline	sideline
crosswalk	crosswalk
somewhere	somewhere
grandstand	grandstand
brainstorm	brainstorm
scrapbook	scrapbook

138

Words in Context
Write the missing spelling words.

At the Park

Challenge
Circle the other compound words in the journal entry.

Sometimes, I walk to the park near my home in the afternoon. I turn left at the second __stoplight__ and then follow the __crosswalk__ into the park. Usually, I walk by myself along the __sideline__ of the __football__ field and find an empty bench __somewhere__ near the woods. I like to blend into the __background__ of the park and watch other people.

Today, I saw a college student sitting under a tree and reading a __newspaper__. There were a few old ladies on another bench looking at a __scrapbook__ filled with photographs of themselves from their childhood. A __classmate__ of mine from school whizzed past them on a __skateboard__.

The bleachers of the __grandstand__ were deserted. The sunlit park was quiet except for the sudden roar of a __motorcycle__ speeding down the __highway__ near the park. I decided to take out a pen and a __notebook__ from my backpack. This seemed like a good time to __brainstorm__ ideas for a story I have to write.

139

Fun with Words
Write the spelling word that completes each sign and includes one word from the underlined compound word.

1. Please don t jaywalk! Use the __crosswalk__ instead.

2. We need to paint the outline of the field to make each end __sideline__.

3. Buy tickets to the fair at the newsstand next to the __grandstand__.

4. Come and enjoy the scenic __background__ of our campground.

5. Shop here for a new bicycle, surfboard, or __skateboard__!

6. Buy one ticket and your teammate or __classmate__ gets one.

7. Make sure you bring your textbook and a __notebook__ to class.

8. The football field and the __basketball__ court are closed.

Words Across the Curriculum
Say each science word. Then, write the word.

1. earthquake __earthquake__   3. waterfall __waterfall__
2. rattlesnake __rattlesnake__   4. heartbeat __heartbeat__

Write the missing science words.

1. A __rattlesnake__ make a warning sound with its tail.

2. During exercise, a person s __heartbeat__ becomes faster.

3. A severe __earthquake__ can destroy buildings, roads, and bridges.

4. A __waterfall__ forms when a stream rushes over rocks that resist erosion.

140

Words in Writing
Write a description of a hobby that you enjoy. Use at least four words from the box.

Answers will vary.

highway	motorcycle	stoplight	grandstand	waterfall
football	newspaper	sideline	brainstorm	rattlesnake
classmate	background	crosswalk	scrapbook	heartbeat
skateboard	notebook	somewhere	earthquake	

Misspelled Words
Read the description. Circle the five misspelled words. Then, write the words correctly.

I like to collect photos and newpaper clippings for my scrapbook. I include articles about my brother s football team. I have a photo of my dad riding his motercycle on the hiway. I also have a photo of myself on the skatboard I got for my birthday.

__newspaper__	__motorcycle__	__skateboard__
__scrapbook__	__highway__	

141

Spectrum Spelling
Grade 4

Answer Key

Write the spelling word that names each number.

1. 19   nineteen
2. 40   forty
3. 11   eleven
4. 13   thirteen
5. 20   twenty
6. 15   fifteen
7. 1,000,000   million
8. 30   thirty

Write the spelling word that is an antonym of each word or phrase.

9. most beautiful   ugliest
10. combined   separate
11. lighter   heavier
12. pain   pleasure
13. sad   happy
14. dryness   moisture
15. answer   question
16. no place   somewhere
17. sunniest   cloudiest
18. most sorrowful   happiest

142

Write the spelling word that fits with each group of words.

19. hockey, soccer,   football
20. million, trillion,   billion
21. rugs, curtains,   furniture
22. republic, country,   nation
23. shape, outline,   figure
24. bicycle, scooter,   skateboard
25. year, decade,   century
26. street, road,   highway
27. safety, preservation,   protection
28. trait, characteristic,   feature

Write the spelling word that is a synonym of each word.

29. ideas   brainstorm
30. setting   background
31. beast   creature
32. dozen   twelve
33. stadium   grandstand
34. place   location

143

Notes

Notes

Notes

Notes